PUBLISHED FOR THE MALONE SOCIETY BY
OXFORD UNIVERSITY PRESS

WALTON STREET, OXFORD OX2 6DP

Oxford New York
Athens Auckland Bangkok Bombay
Calcutta Cape Town Dar es Salaam Delhi
Florence Hong Kong Istanbul Karachi
Kuala Lumpur Madras Madrid Melbourne
Mexico City Nairobi Paris Singapore
Taipei Tokyo Toronto

and associated companies in
Berlin Ibadan

ISBN 0 19 729032 9

Printed by BAS Printers Limited, Over Wallop, Hampshire

HYMEN'S TRIUMPH
BY
SAMUEL DANIEL

THE MALONE SOCIETY
REPRINTS
1994

This edition of *Hymen's Triumph* was prepared by John Pitcher and checked by H. R. Woudhuysen.

The Society is grateful to Edinburgh University Library for permission to edit the text and reproduce pages from its manuscript MS De.3.69.

December 1993 N. W. BAWCUTT

INTRODUCTION

Samuel Daniel's fourth and final play, *Hymen's Triumph*, was performed at Somerset House, Queen Anne's palace in the Strand, on Thursday, 3 February 1614. The play was commissioned by the Queen, and presented at the celebration of the wedding of her friend and chief lady-in-waiting, Jean Drummond, daughter of Patrick, third Lord Drummond, to Robert Ker of Cessford, first Lord Roxborough (created Earl of Roxborough in 1616). The text of *Hymen's Triumph* has survived in (*a*) a manuscript, which is now in Edinburgh University Library, and (*b*) two early printed editions, the first an octavo published in 1615, the second a reprint of the 1615 octavo included in the posthumous collected edition of Daniel's poetry and drama published in 1623. The present edition is a near-diplomatic transcript of the manuscript text.

The Occasion

It is generally assumed, because of its title, and because of the wording of the title-page of the 1615 edition, that *Hymen's Triumph* was written as a wedding play, that is, that Daniel intended it for the marriage of Lord and Lady Roxborough in particular.[1] Another look at the evidence, reviewed below, suggests that this was not the case. *Hymen's Triumph* was a commissioned work, but the decision to play it before the Roxboroughs probably came late in its genesis and composition.

Plans for the Roxborough wedding were made public in November 1613, at the same time as the announcement of another, much more famous (not to say notorious) aristocratic wedding, that of Lady Frances Howard, recently divorced from the third Earl of Essex, to Robert Carr, newly created Earl of Somerset. It is unlikely that these weddings were connected at first, but it appears that they soon became linked, almost competitively, in terms of their respective dates, what they would cost, and who was sponsoring them. According to John Chamberlain, in a letter written to Sir Dudley Carleton on 11 November, the Somerset wedding was originally planned for mid-November, and was to have been celebrated, with King James as guest of honour, at Audley End, the home of the bride's father, Thomas Howard, Earl of Suffolk. Somerset was at the height of his authority and influence over the King—there was even talk of making him a marquis—and with this marriage to Frances he would align himself entirely with the Howard faction at court. Nevertheless, the wedding was not held at Audley End. Queen Anne, although she opposed the royal favourite (and two years later helped to replace him with George Villiers), was

[1] In a recent study Johanna Procter has written that the Queen asked Daniel 'to prepare a play, which was to serve both as compliment to the bridal pair . . . and also a housewarming celebration, as the marriage took place at Somerset House which had been altered under Anne's direction': see '*The Queenes Arcadia* (1606), and *Hymens Triumph* (1615): Samuel Daniel's Court Pastoral Plays', *The Renaissance in Ferrara and its European Horizons/Il Rinascimento a Ferrara ei suoi orizzonti europei*, ed. J. Salmons and W. Moretti (Cardiff and Ravenna, 1984), pp. 83–109 (99).

persuaded to attend the ceremony, and so the wedding, in Chamberlain's words, was 'put of till Christmas and then to be performed at White-hall'.

Elsewhere in the same letter, but not yet linked to the news about Somerset, Chamberlain gives an early (perhaps the first) notice that the 'Lady Jane Drummond is to be maried about Christmas or Twelftide to the Lord of Roxborow'.[2] A little over a week later, when Thomas, Viscount Fenton, wrote to the Earl of Mar, the arrangements had become clearer, and had begun to be coupled:

> I am assured your Lordshipe hes hard that the mariage of Summerset and she that was Ladye Essexx shalbe at Chrissmes. Ther shalbe monye maskes, and it is thocht that on the 12 daye the King shalbe at the Queins houss and geve it sume uther name, and at that tyme Rosborow and Jeane Drummond shall be maried.[3]

By 25 November, although he had nothing to say about the plan to give Somerset House 'sum uther name', Chamberlain was able to report that all the talk at court was

> of masking and feasting at these towardly mariages, wherof the one is appointed on St. Stevens day in Christmas, the other for Twelftide. The King beares the charge of the first, all saving the apparell, and no doubt the Quene will do as much on her side, which must be a maske of maides yf they may be found: and that is all the charge she meanes to be at, saving the brides wedding gowne and the mariage bed, wherin she will not exceed 500li: for she saith her maide Drummond is rich enough otherwise as well in wealth as in vertue and favor.[4]

The weddings had thus become part of the ritual of royal patronage. The Somerset wedding, to be held on 26 December, was planned as the King's gift to his favourite, while the Roxborough one, arranged for 6 January 1614, was to be the Queen's donation to hers. One ceremony was set to open the Christmas festivities at the King's court at Whitehall, the other to conclude them at the Queen's on the Strand.

This symmetry might have been even neater but for the Queen's own plans. She had evidently made it clear that she had no intention of matching the King's largesse towards Somerset, because her own favourite—and here a criticism of Somerset was surely implied—was already rich enough, as wealthy as she was virtuous and attractive (or perhaps 'well-placed at court', if that is what she meant by 'favor'). More important, for Queen Anne the Roxborough wedding was not the only event, perhaps not even the chief one to be celebrated at the end of 1613. The bride, a close friend, might have place of honour at the wedding table, but a still dearer thing to the Queen's heart would have been the completion of four years and more of rebuilding and refurbishment at Somerset House, so as to make this her own royal home, a grand Renaissance palace for a princess of Denmark who had become the Queen (as Daniel described her) of the four nations, England, Scotland, France, and Ireland. The

[2] See *The Letters of John Chamberlain*, ed. Norman Egbert McClure, 2 vols. (Philadelphia, 1939), i. 485–6.

[3] Letter dated 19 November 1613, *Supplementary Report on the Manuscripts of the Earl of Mar and Kellie*, ed. Henry Paton (HMC 61, London, 1930), p. 56.

[4] McClure, *Chamberlain*, i. 487.

reconstruction of Somerset House, begun in 1609, had been extensive and enormously costly. It had involved building a new court, new gallery and new private lodgings, and rebuilding, almost from scratch, the existing ones. By 1613 the work had already cost £34,500, on top of which were the costs for furnishing and equipment—making it in all, according to modern architectural historians, 'one of the most ruinously expensive enterprises of James I's reign'.[5] From the Fenton letter it appears that the renaming of the palace was scheduled for the King's visit on 6 January, and that the Roxborough nuptials were to be part, but no more than part, of the general rejoicing that the Queen's building was finished.

Not all of these things happened as planned. The 'masking and feasting' to celebrate the marriage of Lord and Lady Somerset did begin on 26 December, but the entertainments and gift-giving associated with this, in and out of court, went on well into the new year, up to Twelfth Night in fact. The Roxborough wedding was put off until the night after Candlemas, and the Queen, despite what she had said, managed to spend over £3,000 on it.[6] The King did attend the wedding, and stayed overnight at his wife's new palace, but the name of the building was not officially changed (it had the courtesy title of the Queen's Court until 1617, when it finally became Denmark House, but until then continued to be known as Somerset House). There may have been other changes of plan at this time, perhaps as regards the entertainment provided for the Roxborough wedding. As far back as November, one of the costs Queen Anne had agreed to meet was, as Chamberlain put it, for 'a maske of maides yf they may be found'. It is possible, as E. K. Chambers thought, that this refers to a masque which the Queen had planned, or at least commissioned,[7] presumably to be danced by her maids of honour, or to have as its themes virginity, marriage, and chastity. But Chamberlain may have been reporting nothing more than a vague notion at court, not at all specific, that it would be appropriate for Jean Drummond to be honoured, as a bride, by the other members of the Queen's female entourage. Whatever his exact meaning, Chamberlain's sardonic aside, 'yf they may be found', points to the reputation and moral climate of the court late in 1613, after the Essex divorce: Whitehall, he hints wryly, is not a place where one would expect to find virgins and pure ladies in sufficient numbers even to dance a masque.[8]

It is conceivable therefore that the choice of *Hymen's Triumph* for the Rox-

[5] *The History of the King's Works Volume IV 1485–1660 (Part II)*, gen. ed. H. M. Colvin (London, 1982), pp. 254–61 (255). Daniel describes Anne as the queen of four nations on the title-page of the 1615 edition of *Hymen's Triumph*, STC 6257 (see n. 54 below).

[6] This was the sum which Chamberlain reported to Carleton, 10 February 1614 (i. 507). There is a small difficulty with the date of the performance. According to Finett, the wedding was held on Candlemas, 2 February, but Chamberlain fixes it as 3 February (see i. 504 and 507), the date which is accepted in the present edition: see E. K. Chambers, *The Elizabethan Stage*, 4 vols. (Oxford, 1923), iii. 277.

[7] Ibid.

[8] The divorce and marriage have been recently reassessed by David Lindley in *The Trials of Frances Howard: Fact and Fiction at the Court of King James* (London, 1993): earlier studies are listed in the endnotes on pp. 197–210.

borough wedding was a late one—later than 25 November 1613—and that the play was only taken up as a second option, after a planned masque had been put aside. Preparations for a show of some kind at Somerset House had begun by, at the latest, 4 December (o.s.), when the Italian diplomat Gabaleone reported that the Queen was 'getting ready to present a beautiful masque in her palace' for 'Mrs Drummond's festivities'.[9] It is impossible to say whether this was Daniel's play, or the 'mask of maids' or some other interlude or device. However, if *Hymen's Triumph* was indeed commissioned in late November, and if Daniel had none of it prepared in draft or outline already, he would have needed to write all five acts in a little over ten weeks. Given his facility in writing verse on other occasions, this would probably have been enough time for him to have devised, started, and completed a play as short as *Hymen's Triumph* (which is about two-thirds of the average length of plays intended for the public stage). Such a schedule would not allow him much time to have the play copied, and for the actors to learn their parts, but it would not be insuperably difficult. Moreover, the lacunae in one of the texts, the manuscript—which was presented to the bride on or soon after her wedding day—may indicate that Daniel was still adding new material to the play (the Prologue and three of the choruses) only a short time before the performance. Perhaps this is a sign of just how pressed he was to get everything done by the February deadline.

This account of things, although not impossible, leaves too much unexplained about the type of play *Hymen's Triumph* is, and the place it had in Queen Anne's festivities. The title-page of the 1615 edition describes the play, in slightly ambiguous terms, as 'A Pastorall Tragicomædie. Presented at the Queenes Court in the Strand at her Maiesties magnificent intertainement of the Kings most excellent Maiestie, being at the Nuptials of the Lord *Roxborough*.' The simplest way of understanding this—and no doubt one with which Daniel would have been happy—is that *Hymen's Triumph* was played as part of the Queen's entertainment of the King when he attended the Roxborough wedding at her court (his 'Maiestie, being at the Nuptials'). The phrasing looks clear enough at first, but Daniel has managed not to tell the reader, or not quite to tell him, which event the play was celebrating—was it the King's visit, to grace his wife's magnificent housewarming, or was it the wedding (the 'Pastorall Tragicomædie . . . being at the Nuptials')? The distinction is not unimportant. The *occasion* for performing *Hymen's Triumph* was of course the Roxborough wedding, but the reason that Daniel wrote the play was probably an earlier and quite different commission from the Queen, to provide a suitable celebration for her new palace.

This situation may have been slightly embarrassing for Daniel, although it was not a new thing for him to be caught out, even half compromised, as he negotiated his way between rival patrons. In this case, he had prefaced the

[9] Letter to the Duke of Savoy, quoted from the translation in John Orrell, 'The London Court Stage in the Savoy Correspondence, 1613–1675', *Theatre Research International*, 4 (1977), 79–94 (80).

manuscript text with a dedicatory sonnet to Lady Roxborough in which he assured her that 'this small peece', the play, was 'borne/To be among those rites w^{c} did adorne/Yo^{r} worthy Nuptialls' (ll. 19–21). In the printed text, however, the dedication was addressed to Queen Anne, without any mention of the bride, and the emphasis was entirely on the Queen's munificence. Here, Daniel says of the play, presenting it to Anne,

> what your sacred influence begat
> (Most lou'd, and most respected Maiestie)
> With humble heart, and hand, I consecrate
> Vnto the glory of your memorie:
> As being a piece of that solemnitie,
> Which your Magnificence did celebrate
> In hallowing of those roofes (you rear'd of late)
> With fires and chearefull hospitalitie
> Whereby, and by your splendent Worthines
> Your name shal longer liue then shal your walles:
> For, that faire structure goodnesse finishes,
> Beares off all change of times, and neuer falles.[10]

In this, the only thing which might refer to the Roxborough wedding is 'that solemnitie' in the fifth line, but even if it does—and this is by no means certain—the 'solemnitie' is evidently only part of some larger festival, celebrated 'in [that is, in the course of] hallowing of those roofes' with fires and hospitality. In fact, if the relative 'Whereby' in the ninth line refers to 'solemnitie' (although again this is far from clear), then Daniel is not talking about the wedding at all; it must be Queen Anne's 'Magnificence'—the giving of benefits and the proper use of patronage—which will ensure that her name lives on, not the wedding of one of her lady attendants. The connection between the play and the completion of the palace is made clear in the allusions to the Queen's 'walles' and to 'that faire structure' being finished (her name and 'goodnesse', he declares, will outlive even the fabric of the newly rebuilt Somerset House).

In short, whatever Daniel said privately in the manuscript—which was intended, we shall see, as a personal gift for Lady Roxborough—his public thanks went to Queen Anne for commissioning him to write *Hymen's Triumph* for the formal opening of her palace. Such a commission was entirely what one might expect. Daniel had been one of the Queen's servants at court since 1604, and he had already written a pastoral tragicomedy for her—*The Queen's Arcadia*, performed at Christ Church in Oxford in 1605—and a masque, *Tethys' Festival*, in which she had celebrated the investiture of her elder (and now deceased) son Henry as Prince of Wales. From 1610 onwards, if not before, Daniel received a stipend from the Queen while he was absent from court, an arrangement which allowed him to live down in Somerset while he worked on the second part of his prose history of medieval England, a work he subsequently dedicated to her, in 1618.[11]

[10] 1615 edition, Sig. O2r.

[11] See Pierre Spriet, *Samuel Daniel (1563–1619), Sa Vie—Son Œuvre* (Paris, 1968), pp. 172–3 and n. 37.

We can only guess at the dates when the new play was commissioned, and when Daniel started to write it—possibly as early as 1609, when building work at Somerset House had begun in earnest—but the choice of subject, and who chose it, are less difficult to account for. One of the things for which Daniel was admired by the Jacobean literati, especially perhaps by the Scots, was his deep knowledge of Italian neoclassical writers, and his ease and skill in writing in their vein. *Hymen's Triumph*, even if it failed to please a certain kind of English taste (see below), must have seemed to many of Daniel's contemporaries at court to be an admirable fusion of pure language and neoclassical gracefulness with the structures and ideals of Italian pastoral tragicomedy, particularly Tasso's *Aminta* and Guarini's *Il Pastor Fido*. It was this quality which would have appealed most to Queen Anne herself, who ever since she had arrived in England in 1603 had been acquiring a taste for all things Italian—books, music, gardens, and architecture.[12] There are indications that the new buildings at Somerset House were designed to complement and to preserve the English neoclassicism of the original house, even if they were not inspired by Palladio (this was still a year or so before the appointment of Inigo Jones as Surveyor of the Works).[13] What the Queen probably wanted from Daniel was an elegant complement, in verse and dramatic form, to the Renaissance design and finish of her new palace. Further, the play must have as its themes the delays of love and the triumph of marriage, chiefly because these were the themes of the masters Tasso and Guarini, but also perhaps because the Queen had come to relish her own role, second only to the King's, as a maker of marriages between the English and Scottish aristocracy.[14]

Thus *Hymen's Triumph*, so far as one can tell, was not written specifically for the Roxborough wedding; Daniel's claim, in the manuscript, that it was must be regarded as a pleasantry with the bride (who, as the Queen's confidante, must have known how partial a truth this was). Its appropriateness as a marriage play would have made *Hymen's Triumph* doubly attractive to the Queen when she rearranged the date for the wedding to coincide with the opening ceremony at Somerset House. Since the wedding was set back by over a month, to early February, it is not unlikely that the date for the celebration of the palace was also moved, possibly brought forward a month or two earlier than was first planned. If a change of date was sprung on Daniel quite late in 1613 (in November or December), he may have been pushed to complete the writing, preparation, and rehearsals of the play on time, even if most of it was already in draft. This might explain why the manuscript presented to Lady Roxborough was

[12] Recent studies of Queen Anne's cultural and political patronage include Leeds Barroll, 'The Court of the First Stuart Queen', *The Mental World of the Jacobean Court*, ed. Linda Levy Peck (Cambridge, 1991), pp. 191–208; and Barbara Kiefer Lewalski, 'Enacting Opposition: Queen Anne and the Subversions of Masquing', *Writing Women in Jacobean England* (Cambridge, Mass., and London, 1993), pp. 15–43.

[13] See *The History of the King's Works*, p. 258.

[14] According to Linda Levy Peck, the Queen 'served as godmother and matchmaker to the Jacobean court': see *Court Patronage and Corruption in Early Stuart England* (London, 1990), p. 70.

left incomplete, and why it was copied, with some signs of haste, by two scribes. As he hurried to write new choruses and a prologue for the performance text, and to provide manuscript copies of this for the actors and possibly the Lord Chamberlain too, Daniel would also arrange for another copy to be made for the bride, as promptly as possible, either from his working papers or from an early draft.

Much of this is speculation. More definite are the contrasts between *Hymen's Triumph* and the entertainments written around the same time, but to quite different specifications, for the Somerset wedding. In this context, the most noticeable aspect of Daniel's play is its unusual decorousness of subject-matter and treatment. In the Prologue—not in the manuscript, but published in the 1615 edition—when the god Hymen appears, he is 'opposed by Auarice, Enuie, and Iealousie the disturbers of quiet marriage'. Their promises to '*vndermine*' the marriages Hymen makes, dissolving the '*strongest knots of kindest faithfulnesse*' and producing '*incumbrances*',[15] do anticipate some of the action of the play, but for a court audience early in 1614 such lines must have resonated well beyond the confines of an Arcadian pastoral. The means by which Lady Somerset had got out of her first marriage, with all its incumbrances, and the haste with which she had got into her second, were still the scandal of the moment. Indeed, the themes of Daniel's play—trials of fidelity, deferral of sexual consummation, worship of women, and the prizing of virginity—may have seemed almost quaint, if not prudishly restrained, in comparison with the sexual explicitness and behaviour of Lord and Lady Somerset themselves, and of some of the shows and devices written to celebrate their wedding. Although one must be careful not to invent polarities of taste and moral conduct, there do appear to be marked differences between the outlook and sensibility of *Hymen's Triumph*, played before the Roxborough newly weds, and those of, say, Ben Jonson's *Challenge at Tilt*, performed on 27 December 1613, in which two lewd Cupids debate who is the more sexually energetic partner, Somerset or his bride. In the words of Jonson's most recent biographer, 'this wedding tilt was gamey; but then, so were the bride and groom. Presumably the Somersets, the poor man's Nero and Poppea, wanted to be portrayed in this way. Public misbehaviour was, after all, a way of putting themselves beyond the law, and thus was a sign of their power.'[16]

There were comparable differences between *Hymen's Triumph* and the masques and poems written for the Somerset wedding by Donne, Campion, Chapman, and others.[17] These contrasts were not contrived by Daniel—how could they be, if the writing of the play was in progress well before Lady Somerset was divorced and remarried?—but to the Queen and to some of the courtiers

[15] Sigs. O3v–4r.

[16] David Riggs, *Ben Jonson: A Life* (Cambridge, Mass., and London, 1989), p. 203.

[17] Donne's poems in particular have received close attention: recent studies include William A. McClung and Rodney Simard, 'Donne's Somerset Epithalamion and the Erotics of Criticism', *Huntington Library Quarterly*, 50 (1987), 95–106; Heather Dubrow, *A Happier Eden: The Politics of Marriage in the Stuart Epithalamium* (Ithaca and London, 1990), pp. 178–200; and Patricia G. Pinka, 'Donne, Idios, and the Somerset Epithalamion', *Studies in Philology*, 90 (1993), 58–73.

around her, *Hymen's Triumph* may have offered itself, opportunely, as a snub or a put-down to Lord and Lady Somerset: perhaps it promised to be an antidote, in its sophisticated restraint and simplicity, to the brazenness and vulgar splash of the Somerset wedding and to the panegyrics lavished on the couple personally. What is unimaginable is that Daniel himself intended to slight the Earl of Somerset in this way. Somerset's patronage of him, as we know from several sources, was something for which Daniel was especially grateful, and which he repaid, with considerable loyalty, when the Earl was convicted two years later of the murder of Sir Thomas Overbury.[18] It is true that the Prologue, with its talk of unhappy marriages, may have been written after the annulment of Lady Somerset's first marriage, but there is nothing in it which could be construed as an explicit criticism or reproof of either her or of her husband. Perhaps Daniel's private views on love and marriages at court, beyond their dynastic importance, were not too distant from those expressed at the end of *Hymen's Triumph*, when the foolishness and trials of two fictional characters are related to those of the audience watching the play. You 'faire nymphes', Lidia tells Phillis and Cloris, 'fitly may excuse/these simple slipps'

& know y^t they shall still
haue crosses wth their piles who thus do play
there fortunes wth their loues, as yo^w two did
But yo^w must frame yor countenance thereto
and looke wth other faces then yor owne,
As many els doo heere who in their parts
set shyning lookes vpon their cloudy harts.[19]

The Performance

Not much is known about the staging of *Hymen's Triumph*. For what it is worth, we do know that the day on which it was played, Thursday, 3 February 1614, was so foggy that the sun was barely visible all day, even at noon (which caused one observer, no friend of the Scots at this date, to describe the Roxborough wedding as 'the misty marriage').[20] We know also, on Chamberlain's authority, that the play was staged 'in a litle square paved court' in Somerset House.[21] The actors may have been from a professional company, but if so there is no indication which one it was. (The King's Men, who had acted in the city shows which preceded *Tethys' Festival* in 1610, were frequently at court from November 1613 through to early February, and it was they who performed

[18] Somerset's patronage of Daniel is considered in John Pitcher, *Samuel Daniel: The Brotherton Manuscript, A Study in Attribution* (Leeds, 1981), pp. 67–71. Anne Lancashire has suggested that at least one public stage play (by Middleton) was connected to the scandal over the Somerset marriage: see '*The Witch*: Stage Flop or Political Mistake?', *"Accompaninge the players": Essays celebrating Thomas Middleton, 1580–1980*, ed. Kenneth Friedenreich (New York, 1983), pp. 161–81.

[19] Lines 1903–10 of the present edition (1908 corrected: see p. 70 below).

[20] The phrase is Sir John Holles's: see *Report on the Manuscripts of his Grace the Duke of Portland* (HMC 29 (ix), London, 1923), p. 31. Holles later became a client of Somerset's, who was of course another Scot.

[21] McClure, *Chamberlain*, i. 504.

a play (now lost) at Somerset House on 4 February, when the Lord Mayor presented his congratulations and gifts to the newly weds.)[22] There were at least seven songs in *Hymen's Triumph*, but only one musical setting has come down to us, which does not contain enough evidence to establish the identity of the composer. The gravity of the songs performed for Thyrsis, in I. i and IV. ii (the former sung 'all at flatts' by a boy), might tempt us to suppose that these were set by the poet's brother, the lute composer John Danyel, with whom he collaborated on several occasions, but this can be no more than a guess.[23] From the few bills and payments which have survived, a little can be learnt about the decorative and joinery work done to prepare the palace for the performance and the wedding feast.[24]

There is one description, however, which does give us some idea of how the play was acted and staged. This is in a letter to the Duke of Savoy, dated 6 February (o.s.), from his agent in London, Giovanni Battista Gabaleone. It was Gabaleone who in December had reported that the Queen was preparing a beautiful masque for Jean Drummond's wedding. In his account of the festivities, Gabaleone's main concern, like other diplomats vying for precedence, was to record where he and the various foreign ambassadors had been seated in relation to the royal family. He first describes the wedding banquet, given in the afternoon, then the grand supper which followed it at about six o'clock. 'After supper', he continues,

their Majesties passed into a little courtyard which the queen had had wonderfully transformed with wooden boards . . . and covered with cloth, with many lights, and

[22] Two 'absolute actors', Richard Burbage and John Rice of the King's Men, delivered speeches as Amphion and Corinea in the city's reception of Prince Henry in 1610: see Chambers, *Elizabethan Stage*, iv. 72, and John Pitcher, '"In those figures which they seeme": Samuel Daniel's *Tethys' Festival*', in *The Court Masque*, ed. David Lindley (Manchester, 1984), pp. 33–46 (34–5; and 45, nn. 5–7); for the performance at Somerset House on 4 February, see Chambers, *Elizabethan Stage*, iv. 129.

[23] The one setting is of the song at the end of Act III, '*From the temple to the Boord*'. This appears on Fol. 12a of Bodleian Tenbury Wells MS 1018: see Peter Beal, *Index of English Literary Manuscripts: Volume I 1450–1625*, 2 parts (London, 1980), part i. 206, DaS 52. The setting was first noticed in John P. Cutts, 'Early Seventeenth-Century Lyrics at St. Michael's College', *Music & Letters*, 37 (1956), 221–33 (224–5); Cutts says that 'there can be little doubt' that this is 'the original setting'. The song is unascribed, though a copyist has added at the end 'See Dr Wilsons songs'. It is possible that the song was written by John Wilson (1595–1674), but it is not among his published works, nor has it been found in his manuscripts. The lyrics do have all the hallmarks of Daniel's own writing. Interestingly, John Danyel's song 'Tyme cruell time', a reworking of one of his brother's *Delia* sonnets, is on Fol. 47a of the same manuscript (ibid., p. 229). For John Danyel, see the entry by David Scott in *The New Grove Dictionary of Music and Musicians*, ed. Stanley Sadie, 20 vols. (1980), 5: 233–4, and Gerald Eades Bentley, *The Jacobean and Caroline Stage*, 7 vols. (Oxford, 1941–68), ii. 419–20. In 1603 the brothers presented an interlude together before the King: see Pitcher, 'Samuel Daniel, the Hertfords, and A Question of Love', *Review of English Studies*, NS 35 (1984), 449–62 (459–60). Thanks are due to Dr Christopher Wilson of the University of Reading for guidance over the Tenbury Wells manuscript and John Wilson.

[24] See *Collections Volume X*, Malone Society Collections (Oxford, 1977 (for 1975)), pp. 24–5, under the heading '1 October 1613–30 September 1614', at Somerset House, 'Cxxvij^{li} xv^{s} j^{di} againste the feaste at the marriadge of the Lady Dromonde'; and John Orrell, 'Court entertainments in the summer of 1614: the detailed Works acounts', *Records of Early English Drama*, 1 (1979), 1–9 (6–7).

degrees where all the lords and ladies took their seats. The king sat under a great baldachino; on his right hand sat the queen and on the left the prince, close to the king. On a stool a little further forward on the other side sat the French ambassador, close to the queen. The earls and barons sat on a great bench and I was given a place among them, between the Earl of Essex and the Lord Chamberlain's son. In front of this there were other benches where all the countesses sat, then the French ambassadress, then the baronesses . . . In this same room was performed a pastoral which, for its gestures and its rich costumes, struck me as most beautiful. It had *intermedii* . . . of two most graceful masques performed by young men in very good order. When the pastoral was over everyone retired, and the king slept at the queen's palace.[25]

Gabaleone's account is of limited value, because he could not understand English, but as John Orrell remarks, his 'mention of interludes or intermezzi is especially interesting, as is his description of the special theatre that was erected for the occasion'. His testimony also reinforces the impression that *Hymen's Triumph* was staged very grandly: elsewhere in his letter he calls it a 'grandissimo aparato', a most splendid spectacle.[26]

Nothing more is known about the courtyard theatre. Inigo Jones had designed the stage for *The Queen's Arcadia* and the sets for *Tethys' Festival*, but he was away in Italy until 1615, so he can have had nothing to do with it. Perhaps it was the work of his predecessor as Surveyor, Simon Basil, who had overall responsibility for the rebuilding of Somerset House.[27] The interludes Gabaleone refers to were probably two of the five choruses sung in the performance, one at the end of each act. The manuscript has only the first and third chorus, but the 1615 edition has all five songs, and in the case of the third, at the close of III. v, an extra heading too, 'Here was presented a rurall marriage, conducted with this Song.' It is at this point that Medorus and Charinus, the fathers of Silvia and Thyrsis respectively, withdraw because the 'shepheards festiuals' are about to begin, and their grief for their children has no place at a wedding. In 1615 the third song has six lines:

From the Temple to the Boord,
From the Boord vnto the Bed,
We conduct your maidenhead:

[25] Quoted from the translation by Orrell, 'The London Court Stage in the Savoy Correspondence, 1613–1675', pp. 82–3; there is a copy of Gabaleone's letter in British Library, Add. MS 32023, Fols. 192a–3a, from which further details of the wedding have been taken and translated. The play was mentioned briefly by Philip Gawdy in a letter written to his nephew Framlingham Gawdy soon after the performance: 'To tell yow of my Lo. of Sommersettes marriage, the great gyftes of plate, and the great brauery was ther wth maskes wer very stale, the lyke was at my Lo. of Roxborne marriage, only withe a pastorall' (*Letters of Philip Gawdy*, ed. Isaac Herbert Jeayes (London, 1906), pp. 175–6).

[26] John Orrell, 'The London Court Stage in the Savoy Correspondence, 1613–1675', p. 83; and Add. MS 32023, Fol. 192a. For evidence that Gabaleone could misunderstand entirely what he had seen, see Orrell, 'The Agent of Savoy at *The Somerset Masque*', *Review of English Studies* NS 28 (1977), 301–4 (303).

[27] For Jones in Italy in 1613–15, see the exhibition catalogue *The King's Arcadia: Inigo Jones and the Stuart Court* by John Harris, Stephen Orgel, and Roy Strong (London, 1973), pp. 55–6; for Basil, see *The History of the King's Works*, p. 255.

Wishing Hymen *to affoord*
All the pleasures that he can,
Twixt a woman and a man.[28]

to which the manuscript adds two further lines,

So merely we pass along
w^t o^r ioyfull bridall Song (1346–7)

but ends there, at a discreet point one might say. In another manuscript text of the song, though, the verses continue, not very indelicately, but rather closer to the wedding sheets:

For euer let thy heauenly tapers
on the married brightly shine
And neuer may vnsacred vapours
drowne those glorious flames of thine
O Hymen that our harts & hands dost ioyne
Vntill thy rayes to darkenesse turne
wt^h thy high praise our hearts shall burne
The happy night is now adrest
When loue wt^h beuty must be blest
Let not the Bridgroome bee affraid
Though he encounter wt^h a mayd
Sheele whine, & pale, & start, & cry
And seeme as shee did tremble
But take her & touse her
And tosse her & rouse her
for shee doth but dissemble
And mistrisse Bride thus much to you
I giue in item for tis trewe
A mayden must not bee to coy
In entertayning her wist ioy
Then seeme not straunge in yeelding things
That must not bee denide
But kisse him & hugge him
And vewe him & tugge him
for soe loues knott is tidde.[29]

This version is in a verse miscellany compiled in the early 1630s by one Daniel Leare, who was a distant cousin of the poet William Strode and who was educated at the Middle Temple. We can only speculate on the routes by which the song arrived in this miscellany, with its text and metre very slightly damaged, but there is no reason to doubt that the fuller version was written by Daniel. The text may derive ultimately from one of the parts copied for the actors and musicians who played in the 'rurall marriage'; certainly a text and contemporary musical setting for the first eight lines have survived in yet another manuscript.[30]

[28] Sig. D1v.

[29] British Library, Add. MS 30982, Fols. 35b–36a: in l. 11 ('And neuer may') the 'c' in 'vnsacred' was written as a 't', and in l. 32 'vewe' was first written as 'shewe'.

[30] For the musical setting, see n. 23 above.

The 'rurall marriage' must have been one of Gabaleone's 'graceful masques'. Its position in the play agrees with known practice in other entertainments performed at court, in which the action was interrupted at the end of the second or third act (at a Whitehall performance of *Pericles* in 1619, the audience paused for a midnight supper of sweetmeats and ale between Acts II and III).[31] Situated at the end of III. v, with a Chorus of Shepherds leading the rustic bride and groom to their marriage bed (or perhaps to the threshold of the nuptial bedroom), the interlude would bring into the performance music, sung lyrics, and perhaps dancing to relieve, or at least to modulate, the mood of fine but elaborately wrought sentiment between Sylvia and Thyrsis. The exact way in which this 'marriage' was played we have no way of knowing, but we can guess at it, from Gabaleone's remark that the intermezzi were 'performed by young men in very good order'. Neither the musical setting (if it is the original) nor the lyrics of the rural song (not even 'tosse her & rouse her') suggest anything cacophonous, or rude, or overboisterous—most definitely nothing like the 'hoarse minstrelsy' which Donne, for one, associated with ordinary wedding celebrations.[32] Once again, decorum and modesty prevailed in Daniel's work, even where his contemporaries might have excused (or relished) a fleshier sort of entertainment, perhaps of heavy-footed bumpkins dancing the shaking of the sheets: 'Well-languag'd *Danyel*' probably gave them instead stateliness and the cool flames of wedded chastity.[33] It should come as no surprise that he chose to leave most of the rural song out of the manuscript he gave to the bride, and out of the text of the play he published in 1615.

The emphasis on purity in *Hymen's Triumph*—both in its language and in its treatment of love and sexual passion—evidently bored some people, and probably amused others. John Chamberlain, who had enjoyed *The Queen's Arcadia* at Oxford a decade earlier, attended the performance but thought the play was 'solemne and dull, but perhaps better to be read then presented'.[34] Not long after the performance, in the public stage play *The Hog hath lost his Pearl* by Robert Tailor, published in 1614 (entered in the Stationers' Register, 23 May), there was a confused allusion to Daniel and *Hymen's Triumph*. At the beginning of Act II, Young Wealthy, the stupid son of Lord Wealthy, who hopes to be married to Rebecca, tells her that her father wants them to fix the day. 'What day my lord?', asks Rebecca, to which Young Wealthy replies,

> Why of mariage, as the learned Historiographer writes
> hymens hollidaies, or nuptial Ceremonious rites.[35]

[31] See Chambers, *William Shakespeare: A Study of Facts and Problems*, 2 vols. (Oxford, 1923), ii. 346.

[32] See 'Love's Alchemy', ll. 18–22.

[33] The epithet 'well-languagèd' was applied to Daniel in 1616 by William Browne in *Britannia's Pastorals*, Book 2, Song 2 (p. 37).

[34] McClure, *Chamberlain*, i. 507.

[35] *The Hogge hath lost his Pearl*, ed. D. F. McKenzie, Malone Society Reprints (Oxford, 1972 (for 1967)), [C4]r, ll. 540–1: see pp. vi–viii for the 1613 performance and for the suggestion that the play may have been rewritten.

This must refer to Daniel, whose *First Part of the History of England* was published in 1613 (privately in 1612), but the title of the play has evidently been confused with *Hymen's Holiday*, a (lost) comedy by Rowley acted on the public stage in 1612. *The Hog hath lost his Pearl* was itself played in February 1613, but there are signs that the text was revised before it was licensed and printed over a year later. Young Wealthy's remark looks like an up-to-date, albeit muddled allusion to a smart court entertainment—known only by its title throughout 1614, of course, since nothing else of *Hymen's Triumph* appeared in public until the 1615 edition. What is hard to assess is whether it was the pompousness of Young Wealthy (so keen on 'the best affecting words' and a 'most rare phrase') or Daniel's highbrow, and to some minds, high-falutin style which was being made fun of here.[36]

THE MANUSCRIPT: PROVENANCE

The history of who owned the manuscript is straightforward. As Greg observed, the manuscript gives every sign of being a copy made under Daniel's supervision and presented to the bride, Lady Roxborough, on the occasion of her wedding.[37] In the sonnet on Fol. 2a, written in his own hand, Daniel dedicates the play to Lady Roxborough, and acknowledges that he is grateful for her patronage (presumably she had acted as an intermediary or broker for him at court with the Queen and her household). He adds his signature beneath the sonnet (subscribes it) to affirm what he has written, thus making the manuscript, once Lady Roxborough has received it, a public testimony of thanks. The transaction can only be completed, it appears, when the document has been signed by the client and delivered to the patron (alluding gently perhaps to Lady Roxborough's trade as a courtier, dealing in gifts, benefits, and exchange, the language of patronage).[38] Greg also noted about the dedicatory sonnet that the second line of the heading (that is, 'the Ladie of Roxborough'), although it is in the poet's hand, has been added in a different ink from the rest—as though, as Greg rather spitefully put it, 'Daniel had only learned at the last moment the identity of the lady he had ever longed to honour. Perhaps, however, he delicately waited till the marriage ceremony had been safely performed before addressing the bride by her new title.'[39]

Lady Roxborough owned the manuscript until around 1621, when it was acquired by her distant kinsman, the Scots poet William Drummond of Hawthornden. We know this from a letter written by Drummond to Sir Robert Kerr of Ancram, dated at Edinburgh 7 June 1621, in which Drummond first apologizes for his 'long silence', then tells Kerr, who is in London,

[36] For a convincing account of what Jonson made of Daniel's pastoral style, see Joan Rees, *Samuel Daniel, A Critical and Biographical Study* (Liverpool, 1964), pp. 159–60.

[37] W. W. Greg, '"Hymen's Triumph" and the Drummond MS.', *Modern Language Quarterly*, 6 (1903), 59–64 (61).

[38] The contemporary language of patrons and clients is discussed by Levy Peck, *Court Patronage and Corruption in Early Stuart England*, pp. 12–29.

[39] W. W. Greg, *et al.*, *English Literary Autographs 1550–1650*, 3 parts (Oxford, 1925–32), 3: XXI, n. (*d*).

Though I haue no sute at Court to trouble you with, yet so long as Daniell lastes (who, dying as I heare, bequeathed to you his scrolls) or Done, who in his trauells lefte you his, I will euer find a way of trafficking with yow by letters. Not long since there came to my hands a Pastorelle tragecomedye of Samuell Daniell's, which for her sake at whose mariage it was acted, and to whom it is giuen, I intended to send to the presse. But it both wanting the title and hauing no Chorus, I thought I would first intreate you if there were a more perfect coppye among the Author's papers. Such legacyes, though for the most part they either are contemned or not much made of, yet are found more lasting than what the world esteemes dearer, and to some other this might be a piece of an epitaph, though not to you that builds your fame on higher seated praise.[40]

This manuscript of Daniel's 'Pastorelle tragecomedye . . . wanting the title and hauing no Chorus' is the same one which is now in Edinburgh University Library.[41] Drummond does not say how the manuscript came to him, but he may well have begged it from Lady Roxborough, in the same way that he was trying to beg another one, 'a more perfect coppye', from Kerr. He claims that he wants to publish the play for Lady Roxborough's sake, but his motives were probably more literary and scholarly than personal.[42]

No reply to this letter has been traced, and there is no evidence that Kerr did have another copy of *Hymen's Triumph*, although he certainly had two manuscripts of Donne's (a copy of the poems and of *Biathanatos*), and one of Daniel's too. It is possible that Kerr told Drummond that the 'Pastorelle tragecomedye' had already been published in the 1615 octavo. This edition had all five choruses, as well as a prologue, and it also included the title of the play, together with a dedication in verse to the late Queen. There was no good reason to publish a defective text, and it might prove embarrassing to Lady Roxborough to have the play dedicated to her afresh (which is obviously what Drummond had in mind). Another possibility, whatever Kerr wrote back, is that around this time Drummond learnt that Daniel's brother and his former publisher, Simon Waterson, were gathering the texts for a London edition of Daniel's collected poems and plays, which would include a reprint of *Hymen's Triumph*. Perhaps it was this book, the 1623 *Whole Works*, which persuaded him to give up the plan to print the manuscript (he was certainly interested in this 1623 edition at a later date).[43]

Whatever his reasons, Drummond did not send the manuscript to the press. Instead, he added the title of the play on the first blank page (Fol. 1a), writing it in large (10 mm) capitals, in the same lettering he used for the title he supplied

[40] The letter is addressed to 'the right honorable Sir Robert Karre, knight, gentleman of the Prince's bedchamber': quoted from *Correspondence of Sir Robert Kerr, First Earl of Ancram and his son William, Third Earl of Lothian*, ed. David Laing, 2 vols. (Edinburgh, 1875), i. 24–5.

[41] The manuscript is listed in *The Library of Drummond of Hawthornden*, ed. Robert H. MacDonald (Edinburgh, 1971), no. 1345 (p. 224).

[42] Drummond's estimate of Daniel is discussed briefly in Pitcher, *Brotherton Manuscript*, pp. 16 and 18.

[43] For Kerr's copies of Donne and Daniel, and for Drummond's interest in the 1623 edition, see ibid., pp. 17–18 and 178–84.

to his manuscript of Sidney's *Astrophil and Stella*.[44] In 1626 he gave the Daniel manuscript to the College of King James, afterwards known as the University of Edinburgh, as one of a large number of books and manuscripts he was donating from his private library (including a copy of Daniel's 1602 *Works* folio). Drummond recorded the gift, in his usual handwriting, beneath the title he had written on Fol. 1a. It is reasonable to assume that he wrote the title and the inscription at the same time. In the following year, 1627, in the printed catalogue of his donations to the University, the manuscript was described as dedicated by Daniel 'to the Countesse of Roxbrough./M.S.autog'.[45] The manuscript has remained in the University Library since then. It now has the shelfmark MS De.3.69, and has come to be known as the Drummond Manuscript.

The Manuscript: Binding and Paper

The manuscript is a small quarto-sized volume, bound in seventeenth-century limp vellum, 200 mm × 160 mm, with gold-tooled ornaments on the covers, spine, and edges; the two ties are no longer present, and the holes for the ties have been filled. On the upper and lower covers, there is a central floral lozenge set within an oblong panel of tooled lines, with a fleur-de-lys at each corner, and an outer border of intersecting tooled lines. The binding is conventional, by seventeenth-century standards, but it is probably the original; Drummond must have donated the manuscript to the University Library as he received it from Lady Roxborough, without having it rebound. A large number '23' has been written on the front cover, which tallies with one of the shelfmarks recorded on Fol. 1a, 'P's 23'. The spine of the volume is secured by five sewing bands, and has on it a label with the title '(DANYEL'S HYMENS TRIUMPH. M.S.)', in gold letters on morocco, set round with filigrees and a fleur-de-lys at either end. The gatherings of the manuscript have come loose from the spine, and a rust-coloured thread is visible, together with a small section of pale blue thread, which was probably used to repair the spine at some stage. The binding has been repaired in certain places, before and since the whole volume was restored in 1825. This restoration—which involved adding or modifying the title on the spine, stiffening the vellum and putting a fine glaze over it, and pasting a modern endpaper over the upper and lower inner covers—was done as part of the repair and rebinding of the books given to the University Library by Drummond. The work was supervised by the antiquary and bibliophile

[44] The Sidney manuscript was another of Drummond's gifts to the University Library in 1626: it now has the shelfmark MS De.5.96 (see MacDonald, *Library of Drummond*, no. 1391 (p. 227)). Drummond's inscription on the title-page reads 'ASTROPHEL/and/STELLA written/by/S[r] Philip Sidny/ Knight/[flourish]/Giuen to the Colledge of Edenb./by/W.D.'. A comparison of the large capital letters in this title with those in the words 'HYMENS/ TRIVMPH' confirms that H, E, S, T, R, and P were written by the same hand and in the same ink.

[45] *Auctarium Bibliotheca Edinburgenae, sive Catalogus Librorum quos Guilielmus Drummondus ab Hawthornden Bibliothecae D.D.Q. ANNO 1627* (Edinburgh, 1627), p. 10; the copy of Daniel's 1602 *Works*, STC 6237, which is also still in the University Library, is recorded immediately above the entry for the manuscript (see also MacDonald, *Library of Drummond*, no. 738, p. 190).

David Laing (1793–1878), who arranged that the Drummond books, with a few exceptions, should have commemorative stamps tooled in gold on their new covers.[46] The Daniel manuscript was saved from this, but the stamps—one the Drummond arms, the other a crest of a flying horse with a motto—were added on the inside upper and lower covers respectively.

The manuscript consists of thirty-seven original leaves which measure 197 mm × 157 mm, and eight binder's leaves. The edges of all the leaves have been gilded. At least three watermarks are visible in the original leaves. Two of these—a cockatrice with a shield, and a fleur-de-lys on a shield beneath a crown—have been identified as similar in appearance to Heawood 839 or 840, 1762, and 1768 or 1769,[47] but there is a further watermark, which differs from all of these, and for which there appears to be no close parallel in either Heawood, Churchill, or Briquet: this is a version of the fleur-de-lys with a crown, except that there are two further fleur-de-lys at the base of the shield. Nevertheless, the dates of Heawood's examples, from 1592 to *c.*1616, agree well enough with the likely date for when the manuscript was copied (for the wedding in February 1614). The binder's leaves are arranged four at each end. At the beginning, the pasted-down endpaper and first leaf are from a paper with no chainlines and the watermark 'J Whatman 1825' (which is when the manuscript was restored), followed by three leaves of an older paper which has the watermark 'CL21' and chainlines 25 mm apart. The arrangement appears to be the same at the end, even though the watermarks are not fully visible (working inwards, the Whatman endpaper and leaf is followed by three CL21 leaves).

The manuscript is made up, a little unusually, in three unequal gatherings, the first in five bifolia, the second in six, and the third in eight. The final gathering has detached itself so much from the spine that its order, 23/[36], 24/35, 25/34, 26/33, 27/32, 28/31, and 29/30, is clearly visible, and it is very likely that pages 22/[37] comprise a bifolium too (where [36] and [37] are blank final leaves). This gathering corresponds to Hand A's stint in Fols. 22–35 (see below); at the other end of the manuscript, A probably copied his first stint in a gathering with the order [0]/9, 1/8, 2/7, 3/6, 4/5, although the rebinding and repairs to the spine, and its still fragile state, make it impossible to be sure. On this premiss, Hand B must have copied his text into a gathering in six, 10/21, 11/20, 12/19, 13/18, 14/17, and 15/16. Nothing about the distribution of the watermarks contradicts this explanation, although it is difficult to reconcile it with the numbers written in ink in the right-hand corner of twelve rectos, '2' on Fol. 3a, '3' on 10a, '4' on 12a, '5' on 14a, '6' on 18a, '7' on 22a, '8' on 28a, '9' on 32a, '10' on 33a, '11' on 34a, and '12' on 35a. No fully intelligible pattern emerges when these numbers are set against the present make-up of the gatherings; if they were marks for the binder, one must conclude that they were either ignored or only partly used to put the manuscript together

[46] See ibid., p. 51, and the exhibition catalogue, *William Drummond of Hawthornden (1585–1649): Book collector and benefactor*, by John Hall (Edinburgh, 1985), no. 83.

[47] Edward Heawood, *Watermarks Mainly of the 17th and 18th Centuries* (Hilversum, 1950). The watermarks are identified by Frank Xavier Calvillo in 'A Critical Edition of Samuel Daniel's *Hymen's Triumph*', unpublished Harvard Ph.D. thesis (1979), p. 81.

after it was transcribed. It is difficult to say when the numbering of the leaves of the manuscript, which begins on Fol. 1a and ends on Fol. 35a, was done.

THE MANUSCRIPT: HANDWRITING, COPYING, AND CORRECTIONS

The manuscript is written in three hands; two of them are chiefly secretary, Hand A and Hand B, and one is exclusively italic, Daniel's own hand. The title and the note on Fol. 1a were added by William Drummond, twelve years or so after the manuscript had been transcribed (see above). It has been claimed that there is a fourth hand in the manuscript, which made small corrections and additions to the text: the evidence for this is considered below.

The main work of copying was done by Hands A and B. Greg characterized A's hand as 'that of a professional scribe, small and neat and exceedingly legible . . . of an English character with the introduction of Italian script for names and the like'. Croft described it as 'neat but rather lifeless', and 'typically scribal in its lack of dynamic rhythm'. Hand B, according to Greg, was 'also of an English character, but more influenced by Italian and less neat and clear than [A's] . . . though still very legible'.[48] The distribution of work between the scribes was noticeably unequal. According to the line-count of the present edition (which conforms to Malone Society conventions), the total lines copied were Hand A 1104 and Hand B 760, with Daniel adding 46 lines in his own hand. The copying was divided as follows:

	Fol. 1a		Drummond's title and note, added *c.*1626
Hand A	Fol. 1b	1–16	The Speakers
Daniel	Fol. 2a	17–33	Sonnet to Lady Roxborough
	Fol. 2b		Blank
Hand A	Fols. 3a–9a	34–451	Text of Act I
Daniel	Fols. 9a–9b	452–68	Song of the first Chorus
Hand B	Fols. 10a–21b	469–1229	Text of Act II and opening of Act III
Hand A	Fols. 22a–23b	1230–1338	Text of remainder of Act III
Daniel	Fol. 24a	1339–47	The third Song
Hand A	Fols. 24b–35b	1348–1910	Text of Acts IV and V

Hands A and B can be distinguished in various ways. A does not use catchwords, but B does; B draws a swirl or flourish with his pen at the end of scenes, A does not. A writes speech-prefixes, and the headings for acts and scenes in an italic hand which is noticeably larger, and in some cases much larger, than the secretary hand he uses in the body of the text. There is too an appreciable difference between the dark ink in which he writes the main text, and the lighter but slightly murky ink of many of his italic prefixes and scene headings. A also uses large italics for the song on Fol. 25b, and for many but not all of the personal names in the main text (see Plate 5). On occasions A writes the name of a character in his secretary hand alongside the same name in italic. 'Thyrsis', for example, appears in secretary four times in two lines on Fol. 6b (304–5), but

[48] Greg, '"Hymen's Triumph" and the Drummond MS.', p. 60; P. J. Croft, *Autograph Poetry in the English Language*, 2 vols. (London, 1973), i. 21.

in a large italic on the facing page, Fol. 7a (333: see Plate 1). By contrast, Hand B uses a smaller, more carefully shaped Italian hand for speech-prefixes and headings, and he is almost entirely consistent in writing the characters' names in italic. At the beginning of B's stint, on Fol. 10a, there are no great differences in size and ink between his secretary and italic hands, except perhaps in the headings (see Plate 4). In the course of copying, however, his italic script does become larger and rather more loosely written, especially on Fols. 17 and 18.

A and B differ most significantly in the quality and accuracy of their copying. A's two stints, (1) 1–16 and 34–451, and (2) 1230–1338 and 1348–1910, amount to just over 1100 lines, in which he makes at least thirty slips which remain uncorrected, and over seventy alterations in the course of transcription (adding and interlining letters, writing letters over letters, deletions and so forth). This means that on average he makes a mistake at least once every eleven lines (1100 lines by 100 errors). Putting aside his smudges and over-inking of individual letters, he also makes ten or more ink blots and splodges while copying out these lines. A writes his first stint into twelve full pages, and his second stint, 680 lines, into twenty-four: thus he transcribes the first section at about thirty-four lines per page, and the second at twenty-eight lines per page. B's record is altogether better. He copies his 760 lines in twenty-four pages—just over thirty-one lines per page—but he makes a total of less than ten corrections and unaltered mistakes, an average of under one error every seventy-five lines, and he blots his pages only once or twice. Put simply, Hand A makes seven mistakes for every one that Hand B makes, even though their stints of copying were comparable.

A's work looks even worse if we go beyond these numerical comparisons and consider the seriousness of his mistakes. These were especially bad towards the end of his second stint. In the hundred lines or so on Fols. 33a–35a, he wrote '*Clo.*' for '*Cho.*' (1777), 'lengh' for 'length' (1791), 'vs' for 'as' (1827), 'thy' for 'they' (1833), 'still' for 'skill' (1851), and 'yoman' for 'woman' (1858), but he left all of these errors uncorrected. His eyeslip at 1814, 'eav', went undeleted, even though he copied the full word correctly in the line below ('eaven', 1815). Elsewhere, he omitted the speech prefix at 1668, spelt '*Scen*' as '*Sen*' at 1672, wrongly corrected 'shewed' at 418, and was forced to interline two whole lines he had omitted at 8 and 1516. Moreover, as Calvillo notes, A's misreadings of the text from which he was copying produced lines which were simply unintelligible.[49] At 1231–3, he made Thyrsis recall the time 'wherein I lost the day/And light of comfort that Can never rest/againe to mee', where clearly the correct reading should be, as it is in the 1615 octavo, 'neuer rise/Againe'. At 1328–30, when Medorus is speaking of Thyrsis, Hand A had him ask,

had I but known him in inioying him
as now I doo, to liue, in loosing him
how that had bene mine age,

[49] Calvillo, 'Critical Edition', p. 91.

The correct readings here—those of 1615—are patently 'too late' rather than 'to liue', and 'How blest' rather than 'how that'. By contrast, Hand B is guilty of none of A's grosser errors, and not many of his minor ones either. Where B's text differs significantly from the wording of 1615, most of the variants, as Calvillo puts it, 'seem to result not from misreadings but rather from Daniel revising the text later'.[50] Further comparisons of A and B, in their preferred spellings and punctuation, suggest that in these respects the quality of their copying was about the same.

The question which follows from this is why was B so much more accurate than A? One answer may be that A was working faster than B. The division of work between them appears to coincide with three sets of gatherings, or booklets, in the manuscript—A's first stint in Fols. [0](lost)–9, B's stint in Fols. 10–21, and A's second stint in Fols. 22–37. This indicates perhaps that the scribes started copying at the same time, and that A, after finishing his text on Fol. 9a, resumed work immediately on Fol. 22a. Hand B omits his usual catchword on his final page, Fol. 21b, which may mean that he knew exactly where he was to leave off, once his third of the play was completed; indeed, he may have been given no more text to copy from. If this is true, one might speculate that A made so many errors because he was writing twice as fast as B, copying out two booklets while B did one. Perhaps Hand A was less precise and conscientious than B to begin with, but haste may well have made his work much worse.

This begs another question, of course, which is, why would it have been necessary for the copying to be done so quickly, with the scribes working in tandem? The omission of several songs from the manuscript is the crucial thing here. In A's first booklet, there should be, as there is in 1615, a song at the end of I. i, and one at the end of I. v. Evidently Hand A had neither of these songs in the copy before him, but he left enough space on the recto and verso of Fol. 9, a page and a half, for Daniel himself to write in the second of these, after I. v, '*Love is a sicknes*'. At the end of I. i, however, on Fol. 5b, A left a gap of two lines (between 222 and 223) for a song which in the printed text is fourteen lines long. Whatever instruction there was in the copy which told the scribe to leave a space must have been either unclear, or reflected some uncertainty on the author's part, even as the play was being transcribed, about how long this song would be. On Fol. 7a, at the end of the next scene, I. ii, Hand A left another gap (between 326 and 327), but this time only enough room for one line (see Plate 1). The 1615 edition offers no extra text at this point, so this space was either the result of A's sloppiness and confusion, or yet another indication that parts of the copy supplied to him were not entirely finished or carefully written up.

If we turn to Hand B's booklet, the most noticeable thing about it is not that B omitted the choral song at the end of Act II, but that he left no space for a song at all. Given B's proven care over his text, it is inconceivable that he simply left the song out by mistake. The text he was copying from must have lacked both the song and an instruction to leave a gap for one (in 1615,

[50] Ibid.

the 'song of the second Chorus' has seven lines). The choruses at the end of Acts IV and V, both in A's second booklet, are missing too, but there is adequate space for them—one might say almost too much—on Fols. 31b–32a and from Fol. 36a onwards. Daniel copies part of one song at the end of Act III, in the space left by A at Fols. 23b–24a. There is only one song copied by a scribe in the whole manuscript, the one on Fol. 25b, at the end of IV. ii (1411–16). In this case, Hand A must have received copy which was finished and clearly flagged; the text of the song in 1615 is the same as A's version, and in the same position.

The fact that four of these seven songs are missing from Lady Roxborough's presentation manuscript probably means that Daniel completed them such a short time before the performance that he had no opportunity to have them written in by the scribes, or to copy them himself. He put in the ones which were finished, for Acts I and III, and presented the manuscript at the wedding. The picture which emerges from this, however indistinct, is of the scribes copying the text of the play simultaneously, even as Daniel continued to work on the lyrics of the choruses, and planned whatever music, dances, and action were to go with them (as for the rural marriage at the end of III. v). We can only guess how many manuscripts of the play were needed, beyond the one for the bride, but surely no less than three others—one for vetting at court, one for Daniel to work with (perhaps ultimately printer's copy for the 1615 edition), a master-copy for the actors (who might want further part-copies for individual roles), and so on. If it was left to Daniel to organize all of this, he may well have given the job of making the copies to Hands A and B. It was suggested above that a new, earlier date for the performance may have been sprung on Daniel, perhaps only a couple of months before the wedding. In such circumstances, the poet himself would have to rush to get the prologue, songs, and intermezzi ready for the day, but his scribes, with four or more manuscripts needed at even shorter notice, for rehearsals, rewritings, and presentation, would have rather more to do, copying the body of the text again and again, but without the songs, which the author was due to add at a later date. This explanation, although impossible to prove or disprove, does go a long way to account for the division of labour in the surviving manuscript, and for any haste or at least urgency shown by Hand A, the scribe with most of the work to do.

Little can be said about the actual work of transcription, except that both scribes wrote out their pages in the same way; secretary hand first, with one pen, then italic additions, probably with another (since each script, written correctly, would need a different shaped nib). The procedure would be to copy the main text, leaving gaps within lines and between them, into which the italic names and headings would be written afterwards. Hand A, who was lazier or who had less time than B, only bothered properly about italic for names as speech-prefixes in the left margins, and for characters' names around the beginnings of scenes; his attention elsewhere was intermittent. On Fol. 7a, for example, he copied the dialogue in his secretary hand and left spaces in the middle of the page for the scene-heading, and for the two names 'Thyrsis' and 'Amarillis' immediately below it, which he subsequently added in italic. Above and below this, however, he used secretary for 'Amarillis' three times, and once each for 'Clarendo' and 'Siluia' (323, 325, 339; 327 and 340). Once again B did a better job than this (in 469–98, for example: see Plate 4), but we should take care not to attribute all of A's inconsistency to indifference or idleness, because some of it may be due to the copy from which he was working. This was evidently hard to decipher in places—interestingly enough on Fol. 7a he left gaps at the end of two lines, 335 and 337, just below the spaces for the italic additions. Perhaps the signals for what was to be written in italic were sometimes as unclear as the handwriting itself (how the correct readings were supplied for 335 and 337 is considered below). What is unknown is whether this copy was in Daniel's own hand. If it was, there is a good chance that the whole text was in italic, since there are no signs that he wrote anything at all in a secretary hand in his later years, not even private letters. It is of course entirely possible that the poet had already had parts of the play copied by scribes before Hands A and B began their work, and that what A and B had before them was a largely (if not exclusively) scribal manuscript. The evidence of spellings in the manuscript—comparing Daniel's with those of A and B—has little to tell us in this respect, nor have the layout of the pages and the number of lines per page. The average of lines transcribed on full pages—between 31 and 34—does agree with the average in one of Daniel's own manuscripts (and even with those in his printed 1601/2 *Works* folios), but the half-pages, gaps, and full-page blanks in the *Hymen's Triumph* manuscript compel us to treat these figures very warily; it remains only an intriguing possibility that the scribes copied their stints page-for-page, following the author's layout of the text.

Calvillo claims to have identified a fourth hand, 'of a delicate, Italianate nature', which corrects words 'at eight points' in the manuscript, but only on Folios 7, 8, and 9.[51] He calls this corrector Hand C, although he acknowledges that C may in fact be either Hand A or B, who had switched to an italic script to make the alterations. Calvillo is sure that these corrections were not made by Daniel himself. This account is mistaken in several respects. The number of additions and alterations, beyond those definitely made by A and B in the course of transcription, is in excess of fifty, and these are distributed, rather unevenly, throughout the first quarter of the manuscript, and in the final few pages. More than thirty of the changes are in punctuation. Who made these corrections, in many cases can only be inferred (by the shape of penstrokes, colour of ink, and proximity to other alterations), but there can be little doubt that Daniel himself was responsible for at least ten of them, and perhaps many more. It is not impossible that all but a few of the alterations came from his pen. What follows is a list of the changes which have been observed in the manuscript—excluding those which can be attributed incontrovertibly to A or B as part of their copying—with a note of the points at which the corrected text differs from the reading of the 1615 and 1623 editions of the play (unless noted, the texts of 1615 and 1623 are the same as that of the manuscript, putting aside differences in spelling):

[51] Ibid., p. 81.

209 *see,*] comma smudged, probably in another ink

321 *repossessed*] the scribe wrote *repossed*; another hand struck out *d* and interlined *ssed* in italic above the deletion, with two carets

335 *sex ?*] added in italic hand

337 *their wills,*] added in italic hand

349 *temporize*] added in italic hand

392 *Ph.*] added in italic hand; not in 1615 and 1623

393 *haste*] *e* perhaps added by another hand (*hast* in 1615 and 1623)

394 *haste*] *e* added by the hand which added 392 *Ph.* (*hast* in 1615 and 1623)

434 *your*] interlined in italic hand, above a caret

his] interlined in italic hand, above deletion of *ther*, with a caret

448 *aparte*] added in italic hand after deletion of *apast*

450 *I'le*] interlined in italic hand above deletion of *will*, with a caret; no correction in 1615 and 1623 (= *I, yet, will*)

466 *it,*] comma added in darker ink, or made with a sharpened nib

467 *it,*] comma added in darker ink, or made with a sharpened nib; comma appears to be misplaced here, but correctly positioned in 1615 and 1623 (= *enioyd, it*)

473 *(Who . . . rough)*] brackets added by another hand, in the same colour of lighter brown ink used by Daniel on the facing page, Fol. 9b, to transcribe the First Chorus (the same ink was used for the other alterations in 473–4); no brackets in 1615 and 1623 (= *VVho . . . rough,*)

bee,] interlined in italic hand above deletion of *were* (cancelled with a single horizontal stroke), with a caret; the same hand added a comma after the deletion (1615 and 1623 = *be*)

474 *priz'd,*] comma added by another hand

491 *loue,*] comma added in lighter brown ink of alterations of 473–4; so too for the comma added after 492 *proue* (1615 and 1623 = *prooue;*), 494 *desires* (1615 and 1623 = *desires.*), 496 *sustaine* (1615 = *sustaine:* 1623 = *sustaine;*), 499 *heare* (where the comma was added below a stop, to make a semicolon; 1615 and 1623 = *heare.*), 500 *resorte*, 511 *happines* (1623 = *happinesse;*), 528 *lost*, perhaps 531 *slaues*, and 532 *world*. The same lighter brown ink was used for the comma after 565 *sad* (1615 and 1623 = *sad?*), and perhaps at 569 for the head of the question mark in *you?*

1524 *serv'd*] added in secretary hand

1600 *talke,*] comma added in lighter brown ink

1688 *tragidie,*] comma added in lighter brown ink; 1615 and 1623 have *tragedie;*

1691 *proportion'd*] apostrophe perhaps added in lighter brown ink

1693 *What?*] *?* written over stop in lighter brown ink (1615 and 1623 = *What*), which was also used for the question mark written over a stop at 1695 *mee?* and at 1696 *nimph?*

1699 *harmes,*] comma added in lighter brown ink; 1615 and 1623 have *harmes*

1711 *thereby,*] comma added in lighter brown ink; 1615 and 1623 have *thereby*

1727 *stares, and*] comma added in lighter brown ink by another hand, which wrote *and* over two indecipherable letters (1615 and 1623 = *stares and*), and which also added a comma in the same ink after *th' ayre*

1728 *that's*] italic *s* written over secretary *s* (letter shape '6') by another hand, which added the apostrophe

1734 *transformd?*] *?* added over stop in lighter brown ink

1736 *speeke.*] stop added in lighter brown ink
1737 *sownes,*] comma added in lighter brown ink
1740 *shepcot*] *e* altered from *i* by another hand; 1615 and 1623 have *sheep-cote*
1741 *agayne,*] comma added in lighter brown ink; 1615 and 1623 have *againe.*
1773] line crossed through with two or three horizontal strokes in the brown ink used by the italic hand which altered 1774; not deleted in 1615 and 1623
1774 *And*] interlined above deletion of *Yet* in italic hand, with a caret; no correction in 1615 and 1623, which retain *Yet*
1775 *fellow,*] comma added by another hand, in the ink of 1774 *And*
1778 *newes,*] comma added by another hand (1615 and 1623 = *newes.*), probably in the ink of 1774 *And*

Three things should be noted from the outset. First, that none of these penstrokes or punctuation marks looks anything like those in Drummond's handwriting on Fol. 1a, or in his other papers and letters. Second, that whoever made these corrections—one person, or two, or more—evidently wrote them in without consulting either of the early printed editions, 1615 or 1623. Third, that some of the added words were written into spaces left blank by Hand A. One of these, 'serv'd', the final word in 1524, is in a quite large, florid secretary hand, with a size and angle of hand which resemble those of A's italic. If 'serv'd' was indeed A's, he may have added it at the same time he wrote the two italic speech-prefixes at 1532–3 (further up the page at 1516, he interlined a full line in secretary, but the ink indicates that this was in the course of copying the whole passage, rather than afterwards). The italic additions in A's first stint, on Fol. 7 at 335, 337, and 349, cannot possibly be his (the first two are illustrated in Plate 1). The hand is much smaller than A's, and the letters are made altogether differently. It is conceivable that the words were added by Hand B, who was checking over A's first booklet, filling in gaps, and making corrections. Three pages on, the same hand, whether B's or not, crossed out A's mistake at the end of 448, 'apast', and wrote '*aparte*', and may have made the corrections at 434 too (see Plates 2 and 3). One odd thing about this correcting hand is that it added something at 392 which was apparently unnecessary, the speech-prefix '*Ph.*'. This is the only occasion in the whole manuscript when the first line of a scene is given a prefix. Perhaps the corrector made a mistake, or perhaps the copy he was consulting had this reading; he certainly examined the text very closely, even punctiliously, to the extent of adding a single letter *e* to 'hast' in 394 (and perhaps at 393 as well).

Hand B's italic, in his own stint, is generally rather more formal than any of these additions, with each of his letters spaced and written separately (for examples, see Plate 4). However, given that several of the corrector's letters are interlinear and made to suit the scale of the surrounding secretary hand, it is quite possible that these were indeed added by B, who was writing quickly. One alternative is that the corrector is another scribe altogether. If so, his task was confined to comparing and correcting A's first stint against the copy, since there are no signs of his hand elsewhere in the manuscript after Fol. 9a. The possibility that some of these corrections were made by the author himself is worth canvassing. P. J. Croft described Daniel's hand as a 'dashing and stylish Italic', with letter shapes which are easily recognizable. The poet uses, he says,

> both Italian and Greek *e* but his most characteristic form was evolved under the stress of speed and conforms to no orthodox type of *e* though it closely resembles the numeral *2* and a type of *r* still in use whose ancestry goes back to the medieval period: Daniel's habitual use of this form to represent *e* . . . is a personal eccentricity. Daniel's final *s* often descends well below the baseline: similar forms occur in other Italic hands of the period and suggest the influence of the looped termination used for final *es* in contemporary Secretary, itself sometimes influenced by the sinuousness of Italic final *s*.[52]

The example of Daniel's hand from which Croft started is in fact the one on Fol. 9a of the *Hymen's Triumph* manuscript (see Plate 3), and he says of the italic alterations at 448 and 450 that these 'are in a third hand', that is, they are neither Daniel's, nor Hand A's. This is probably incontestable for the one at 448 (see above), but it is less easy to put aside '*I'le*' at 450. One hesitates to take issue with Croft, but the slope, letter shapes, and ink of '*I'le*' are not at all unlike Daniel's; even the letter *e*, which looks little more than a splodge, may have been formed as a numeral *2*, one of the characteristic features of the poet's hand, according to Croft. There is also the question of why this alteration was made at all. Before the manuscript was corrected, 450 read, quite simply,

> and yo^{w} shall finde, I yet will set yo^{w} free.

a meaning preserved in the 1615 text, despite two extra commas ('shall finde, I, yet,'). The manuscript correction changes the second half of the line, however, to mean either 'I yet, I'll set you free', or perhaps 'aye yet, I'll set you free'. None of these versions is altogether satisfactory, but it is easier to believe that it was the poet rather than a scribe who attempted to improve the metre and to clarify the sense of the line. The same thing may be true of the deletions and interlineations at 434, where the line at first was:

> loue takes for misprision of ther powre.

This is defensible as an original version, metrically ('misprision' as four syllables) and in meaning (Phillis has deprived the foresters and herdsmen of 'ther powre', rather than Love of his). The italic interlineations—'*your* misprision' and '*his* powre'—were either the author's late alterations, or scribal corrections needed to restore the reading of the copy (1615 has 'your' and 'his'). In this

[52] Croft, i. 21; the facsimile of Fol. 9a is on the facing page. Further examples of Daniel's italic hand are illustrated in plates or facsimiles in the following: (1) autograph letter (1605) in 'post 4to' copies of *The Complete Works in Verse and Prose of Samuel Daniel*, ed. A. B. Grosart, 5 vols. (no place, 1885–96), page facing I. xxii; (2) portion from autograph letter (1605); autograph stanza from *Panegyric Congratulatory* (1603); and Fol. 9a of *Hymen's Triumph* in Greg, *English Literary Autographs*, 3: XXI; (3) Fol. 9 of *Hymen's Triumph* in *English Poetical Autographs*, ed. Desmond Flower and A. N. L. Munby (London, 1938), facsimile 5 and p. 1; (4) holograph corrections to stanzas in *The Civil Wars*, ed. Laurence Michel (New Haven, 1958), pp. 43 and 46; (5) Fol. 9 of *Hymen's Triumph* in Rees, *Samuel Daniel*, between pp. 158 and 159; (6) autograph stanzas from *Panegyric* in Beal, *Index*, p. 200; (7) autograph stanza from *Panegyric*; holograph additions to appendix of prose sources (?1618) in Pitcher, *Brotherton Manuscript*, p. 180; and (8) autograph letter (?1602) in Pitcher, 'Samuel Daniel's Letter to Sir Thomas Egerton', *Huntington Library Quarterly*, 47 (1984), 55–61 (57).

case the handwriting is rather less like Daniel's italic, but there are still similarities (see Plate 2).

These are instances which can be debated, but the corrections at 473 are unequivocally Daniel's. Five lines into Hand B's stint, on Fol. 10a, Daniel noticed a slip, either his own or the scribe's. He deleted 'were', interlined '*bee*' above a caret, using his numeral *2* for *e*, and then placed brackets around the whole line (see Plate 4). He made these alterations in the same lighter brown ink he had used to add the choral song on the facing page, Fol. 9b. Presumably he did this when the manuscript was already made up as a single book, rather than still in three separate booklets. He copied in the song, glanced across the opening, Fols. 9b–10a, and put right the mistake at 473. His eye and pen travelled down the page, and he added commas in the same ink at the end of lines 474, 491, 492, 494, and 496. He turned over the page, to Fol. 10b, made four further changes in punctuation, then two on the next page, and two more on the one following (Fol. 11). After this he appears to have lost interest, or (less likely) he was satisfied with everything Hand B had done. It is impossible to be sure that all of this extra punctuation is Daniel's, but other ways of explaining it are less than plausible (that it was added by a diligent scribe using the same ink, or by Lady Roxborough, or by a later reader in the University Library). Much the same thing can be said about the changes at 1600, in a line at the top of a page (Fol. 29a), and those at 1688, 1691, 1693, 1695, 1696, 1699, 1711, 1727, 1728, 1734, 1736, 1737, 1740, and 1741, all of which are in the final three pages of Act IV (Fols. 30b–31b), immediately before the blank page into which the poet should have written another choral song (Fol. 32a). The reason that Daniel paid particular attention to these pages is probably connected to the changes forced on him in Fols. 32b–33a. What he found there was that when the binder had trimmed the pages of the manuscript, ready for presentation, he had cut away the bottom of Fol. 32, and with it the lower half of 1773. Daniel crossed out 1773 in his usual brown ink, and replaced 'Yet' in 1774 with '*And*', thus making a new join, in grammar and sense, between 1772 and 1774. He made two further small changes immediately below, at 1775 and 1778. At this point he may have turned back through a few of the preceding pages, making minor changes, but again not in any systematic or sustained way.

The number of corrections *not* made by Daniel in this list may in fact be quite small—perhaps no more than the ones around 335, and at 349, 392, 434, and 448 (the correction at 321, although only part of a word, has Daniel's letter forms for *s*, *e*, and *d*: see Plate 1). If the remainder is indeed Daniel's, the list makes clear just how concerned the poet could be with the minutiae of his text—with commas, question marks, spellings, and letter shapes (in 1728 and 1740, for example). It also shows that his attention to detail could be patchy and unsystematic, and that on occasions he could even be inaccurate. At the close of the choral song on Fol. 9b (466–8), he first wrote (of love), in the lighter brown ink,

more we inioy it more it dyes
yf not inioyd it sighing cryes
Hey ho.

He then added a comma after '*inioy it*' and '*inioyd it*', either in a darker ink or when he had sharpened the nib of his pen. According to Croft, Daniel intended something special by this. 'In the poet's view', he writes,

> a lyric of this kind clearly did not require conventional punctuation and, apart from the full point at the end of each stanza, his only punctuation here consists of the commas . . . [in 466 and 467]; the manifestly ungrammatical punctuation [in 467] . . . shows that Daniel is here using the comma, as its medieval precursor the *virgula* had been used, to mark the caesura.[53]

This may be so, but it is worth noting that in the 1615 printed text the comma at 467 was moved to a grammatically correct position ('*enioyd, it sighing cries,*'). Perhaps Croft's explanation was altogether too elaborate, and on Fol. 9b Daniel simply added the comma in the wrong place, positioning it, rather mechanically and carelessly, beneath the other '*it,*' in the line above.

The Manuscript and the Edition of 1615

A critical edition of *Hymen's Triumph*, prepared by John Pitcher, will appear in the four-volume Oxford English Texts edition of Daniel's complete poetry and drama, to be published by the Clarendon Press over the next few years. This edition will be based on the 1615 printed text, and will contain a full textual introduction and commentary. What is offered here is a brief summary of what is known about 1615, and an outline of its relationship with the manuscript.

Hymen's Triumph was entered in the Stationers' Register on 13 January 1615, almost a year after the Whitehall performance. It was published as an octavo edition by Francis Constable, a young publisher who was a few months out of his apprenticeship. Excluding private printings, this is the only book of Daniel's which was not published by Simon Waterson (or Waterson with Edward Blount). It is possible that Constable was given the chance to publish the play, as his first book, because of business connections he and Waterson had with the Cambridge master printer, John Leggatt; as Calvillo has shown, it was Leggatt who printed *Hymen's Triumph*. Calvillo has also demonstrated that the book was set by one compositor—who used two skeletons and sets of running-titles—and that stop-press corrections were made in two of the five sheets, in signatures D and E. Three copies of the book have survived, two in the British Library, one in the Huntington Library: the one given to the Bodleian Library, as part of its arrangement with the Stationers' Company, seems to have disappeared. The version of *Hymen's Triumph* in the 1623 *Whole Works* was set from the 1615 edition, with a few corrections and several mistakes.[54]

[53] Croft, *Autograph Poetry*, i. 21.

[54] The 1615 octavo is STC 6257. For the SR entry and location of copies, see Greg, *A Bibliography of the English Printed Drama to the Restoration*, 4 vols. (London, 1939–59), no. 325. For Francis Constable; Leggatt as printer (an identification the revised STC agrees with); identification of compositor; sequence of printing; press-corrections; and 1623 as a reprint, see Calvillo, 'Critical Edition', pp. 95–6, 97–100, 104–5, 107–8, 111–12, and 113–15 respectively. The Bodleian copy of the 1615 edition is recorded in Thomas James, *Catalogus Vniuersalis Librorum in Bibliotheca Bodleiana* (Oxford, 1620), p. 157.

The 1615 text differs from the one in the manuscript in several ways, some of which have been mentioned above. It has a forty-line dedication to Queen Anne, a fifty-eight line prologue, and seven songs, five of them choral. The manuscript, by contrast, has a sonnet to Lady Roxborough but no prologue, and three of the songs. The manuscript has five complete lines which are not in 1615. Two of these are the couplet at the end of the third chorus (the song of the rural marriage), and the others are single lines at 799, 1259, and 1654: only the first, 799, appears to have been left out by mistake by the printer (1773, the line cut in half by the binder and crossed out by Daniel, is present in 1615). As well as these large differences, there are, according to Calvillo, 'over one hundred substantive variant readings' between the texts.[55] Some of these were mistakes made by the scribes, others by the 1615 compositor; still others were caused by errors and omissions in the copy (or copies) from which the manuscript was transcribed and the printed text was set.

Greg, comparing the two texts, concluded that the manuscript represents 'the original in its uncorrected state on the whole more accurately than the octavo does the same original after it had undergone revision'.[56] Calvillo agrees with this, but he argues further that Daniel 'made his revisions' of the play 'on the foul papers which had served as the copy' for the manuscript, 'and then made or had made a fair copy' for the press. The assumption in both cases is that the manuscript was copied from an 'original'—Calvillo takes it to be 'foul papers' or a working draft—which Daniel corrected and supplemented. Greg thought that 'the original' served as printer's copy (or at least he implies this), but Calvillo claims that another copy, a fair draft, was made from it, and it was from this that the octavo was set. This must be so, he says, because the 'foul papers' would have been in such a mess after Daniel had revised and added to them that they would have been unsuitable for the press. Further, the mistakes in the manuscript—misreadings and blank spaces in many places—are fewer in number and seriousness than in the octavo, so the compositor's copy 'must have been cleaner' than the one the scribes had before them.[57]

These conclusions are questionable. It is not yet established that Hands A and B were working from the same quality of copy—perhaps some of it was in Daniel's hand, the rest in a scribe's—nor is it self-evident that Daniel would send his revised 'original' to the printer, nor even that the sequence proposed by Calvillo (working papers, then revised working papers, then a fair draft for the printer) is inherently likely—why not working papers, then draft, then revised draft to the printer? Economy of hypothesis, which is the principle that Greg and Calvillo appear to be observing, may be appropriate for the printing of public stage plays but perhaps quite unsuitable for the social circumstances of a court play written by a courtier poet. As to the 1615 compositor, his setting of the last few lines of the text hardly confirms Calvillo's confidence in his accuracy. At 1907–8, the manuscript reads

But yo^{w} must frame yor countenance thereto
and looke wth other face then their own

55 Calvillo, 'Critical Edition', p. 90b.

56 Greg, '"Hymen's Triumph" and the Drummond MS.', pp. 61–2.

57 Quotations in this paragraph are from Calvillo, 'Critical Edition', pp. 102–3.

The second half of 1908 should read 'faces then yor owne', but the compositor, missing this obvious blunder, printed 'faces then their owne'. The significance of Daniel's alterations to the manuscript—in punctuation and spelling as well as wording—has also to be weighed in this, especially since (if they are his) most of these corrections were not incorporated into the copy from which 1615 was printed.

A full review of the evidence must be deferred for now, but it may be that the views of Greg and Calvillo will in time require considerable modification. What is not in doubt is that the manuscript and the octavo are collateral texts. The version of the play in the manuscript was revised and corrected, and the changes, or most of them, may well have been completed by the time of the performance. The octavo was not set from an acting copy or a prompt-book. Whatever his haste in writing the play, Daniel was in no rush to have it published. It may be that we should seek to explain his delay—well over twelve months—not in terms of a printing history, but against the background, once more, of the impending crisis at court during 1614 and 1615 over the conduct of Lord and Lady Somerset.

Editorial Conventions

This is a page-for-page, near-diplomatic transcription, in which the following conventions have been observed. Square brackets enclose deletions, except those around folio numbers and act and scene numbers ([II. ii.][Fol. 12b] etc.). Angle brackets enclose material which other causes (paper damage, blotting) have removed or made difficult or impossible to decipher. In such cases, dots indicate illegible characters (thus <.>). Interlineations of words or full lines are enclosed within half brackets (thus 1396 ⌜scarce⌝), but interlined letters are not; all interlineations are recorded in the textual notes. Carets are not printed, but their presence is noted in the footnotes. Differences in the sizes of italic hand have been regularized: one large size for headings, names, etc. (in both scribal stints), and a smaller one, the same size as for the main text in roman, for the additions listed above, pp. xxvi–vii. Words are printed in italic where all or most of the letters are clearly written in an italic hand.

Each line of text—including cancelled lines, act and scene divisions, speech-prefixes, and stage-directions—is numbered separately. Catchwords, decorations, and interlineations of one or two words are excluded from the line count. Also excluded from the count is the numbering of the leaves, and the numbers which were perhaps intended for the binder (the latter are not printed in the text, but recorded in the textual notes). Numbering for the text is continuous, and begins with the list of Speakers on Fol. 1b (since the writing on Fol. 1a is Drummond's). Omitted from the text, but noted in the collations, are decorative flourishes and the various markings not intended as part of the transcript (ink blots, pen marks, etc.). The position of elements of the text such as speech-prefixes, headings, catchwords, and indented text is reproduced as exactly as type permits, but other features are normalized.

As with any transcription, several shapes require editorial decisions, especially in distinguishing between majuscule and minuscule forms (for example, 330 'my' and 493 'you': see Plates 1 and 4). This is also true for the suspension of letter forms, where the intention to raise a letter is not always certain, and where the letter is not always fully formed (especially *w* in 'yo^{w}': compare examples in Plate 1, 429 and 438, against those in 435–7). Superscript letters have been printed the same size as the remainder of the text. Marked irregularities in word-division are recorded in the collations. Apostrophes are printed even when they appear to be superfluous (as in 1307 'hum'ble'; 1668 'me't'; 1818 'loo'ke'), and regularized where they are needed but have been misplaced (so 'rul'd' at 520, instead of 'ruld'' as written). The position of punctuation above or below the line has been normalized. Marks made when the scribe allowed his pen to rest, inadvertently, on the paper, in the course of transcription (for example, 608–9 'I would./Haue') are omitted where it is clear that the point was intended neither as punctuation nor to mark a caesura. The longer strokes or virgules which the scribes used to end lines are printed in the text. The abbreviations for *er*/*ar*, *per*/*par*, *pro*, *us*, and *que* have been expanded, and shown in the text in italic (thus 185 'Reliq*ues*', 1552 'p*er*ceuing'). Other contractions and tildes, and the circumflex over *o*, are printed as they appear in the manuscript. Long *s* has been lowered and terminal *s* rendered as *s* rather than *es*, even where the letter resembles the common abbreviation for *es*/*is*; ligature *æ* has been retained.

Scribal mistakes are recorded in the textual footnotes, with the reading of the 1615 edition, where this is obviously the correct one, given to the right of the lemma. Thus, on Fol. 3a, in the note '53 *trurnd*] for *tournd*', the reading '*tournd*' is that of 1615. Readings from 1615 are also noted, selectively, where there are words missing in the manuscript, or mistakes which might reflect earlier versions; a full-scale collation has not been attempted. An asterisk in the textual footnotes indicates that the reading in question—a correction or added word or punctuation mark—is listed and discussed on pp. xxvi–vii; these alterations have not been attributed in the collation notes, even though some of them (perhaps most) were made by Daniel himself.

The pages in Plates 1–5 have been reproduced four-fifths full size.

shall I repeat the same againe to thee?
or els will thou rehearse it unto me,
that I may know thou hast it perfect, Boy.

Cla. No, that needs not, be sure I will repeat
what you enjoyne me in most earnest sorte.

Clo. Oh doo good Boy, although I feare it will
availe me little, for I doubt his hart
is repossest with an other loue.

Cla. Another loue, who may that bee I pray?

Clo. With Amarillis. I haue heard, for they
are thought will in the end, make up a match.

Cla. With Amarillis. well, yet will I go.
and trie his humor whether it be so.

Clo. Go good Clarindo, but thou must not faile
to worke effectually for my availe,
And doe not stay, returne with speed good Boy,
my passions are so great, endure delay.

Act. 2. Scen. 3.

Clarindo. Sol.

Thyrsis in loue with Amarillis. then
in what case ame I? what doth availe
this altred habit that belyes my sex?
what bootes I haue escap't from Pyrats hands,
and with such wiles to haue deceiued their wills,
if I returne to fall on worse ills?
In loue with Amarillis? is that so?
Is Silvia then forgot that hath indur'd
so much for him? doo all theis miseries
caused by his meanes, deserue no better hire?
was it the greatest comfort of my life

PLATE 1: EDINBURGH UNIVERSITY LIBRARY MANUSCRIPT, De.3.69, FOL. 7a, HYMEN'S TRIUMPH, LINES 314–43 (HAND A, AND CORRECTIONS)

Cla. Beleeue me Phillis I doe pitty thee,
and mone, lament thy error; so fare well.

Ph. And art thou gon hard-harted youth? hast thou
thus disappointed my desires, & least
my shame t'afflict me worse then my love?
Now in what case am I, that neither can
recall my modestie, nor thee againe?

Ah were it now to doe againe, my passions should
haue smotherd me to death, before I would
haue with the smallest sparkle of my flame;
But it is done, & I ame now vndon.

Ah hadst thou ben a man, & had that part
of understanding of a womans hart
my words had ben vnborne, only mine eyes
had ben a tongue enough to one were wise.
But this it is to loue a Boy, whose yeares
conceaues not his owne good, nor weighs my teares,
but this disgrace I iustlie haue deserud

Scen. 5.

Lidia. Phillis

Lid. So Phillis, haue you, and y'are rightly serud.
Haue you disdaynd the gallanst fforresters
And brauest Heardsmen all Arcadia hath?
and now in loue with one is not a man?
Assure your selfe this is a iust reuenge
loue takes for your misprision of his power:
I tould you often there would come a time
when you would ~~laugh~~ sure be laugh'd for such a ryme,
but you would laugh at me as one you thought
conceiud not of what mettaile you were wrought

So this you whoe would wonder any Nimph
could euer be so foolish as to loue?

PLATE 2: FOL. 8b, LINES 409–40 (HAND A, AND CORRECTIONS)

9

who is so foolish now? Ph. peace Lidia peace
Add not more greif t'a hart that hath to much,
Do not insult upon her misery
whose flame, God wott, needes water & not oyle.
Thou seest I ame undon, caught in the toyle
of an intangling mischeif, tell me how
I may recover, and unwinde me now.

Lid. That doth require more time, wee will ~~apart~~ aparte
consult thereof, be you but ruld by mee.
and you shall finde I yet ~~will~~ shalle set you free.

Exeunt.

The Song of the first Chorus.

Love is a sickness full of woes
All remedies refusing
A plant that with most cutting growes
most barrayne with best usinge
why so
More we inioy it more it dyes
If not inioyd it sighing cryes
Hey ho.

PLATE 3: FOL. 9a, LINES 441–60 (HAND A, DANIEL'S HAND, AND CORRECTIONS)

10

Actus. Secu: Scæn. 1.

Siluanus. Dorcas. Montanus.

In what a meane regard are wee now held
wee actyue and laborious forresters,
who though o' living rurall ~~were~~ bee and rough
yet heretofore were wee for vallo[r] prizd,
And well esteemd in all good companies.
Nor would the dayntiest nymphes that valleys haunt
or feilds inhabite, ever haue dispizd
our siluane songs, nor yet our playne discourse.
But gracefully accepted of our skill
And often of our loues, when they haue seene
how faithfull and how constant wee haue bene.
Dor. Its true Siluanus, but you see the tymes
Are altred now, and they see dainty growne
By being adord, and wood, and followed so
of those unsyncere amourous heardsmen, who
By reason of their rich and mightie flocks
Supplie their pleasures wth that plenteousnes
As they disdaine our playnenes, and doo skorne
our companie, as men rude and ill borne.
Sil: well so they doo. but Dorcas if you marke
how oft they doo miscarrie in their loue,
And how disloyall their fine heardsmen proue:
you shall perceiue how their aboundant store
Payes not their expectation, nor desires,
witnes their groues wherin they oft deplore
The miserable passions they sustaine.
And how perfidious, wayward, and unkinde
They finde their loues to be. wth wee who are

The.

PLATE 4: FOL. 10a, LINES 469–98 (HAND B, AND CORRECTIONS)

Th. Doo good Palemon go yor way, farewell
And yet Palemon stay, perhaps you may)
by charmes you haue caused sleepe to close mine eyes
for you were wont, I doo remember well
To sing me Sonnets wch in passion I
composed in my happier dayes when as
her beames inflamed my spirits, wch now are set
And if you can remember it, I pray
Sing me the Song, wch thus begins: Eyes hide my loue.
wch I did write uppon her earnest charge
she gaue vnto me to conceale or loue.

The Song. Eyes hide my loue, and doo not shew
to anie but to her my notes
who onely doth that Cypher know
Wherewth wee pass our secret thoughts
bely your lookes in others sight
and wrong yor selues to doo her right.

Pal. So now shee sleepes, or else doth seeme to sleepe
But how so ere I will not trouble him

Scen. 3.
Clarindo. Thyrsis.

See where shee lyes whome I so long to see
Ah my deare Thyrsis take thie quiet rest
I know thou needst it, sleepe thy fill, sweet loue
let nothing trouble thee: be calme o windes
Bee still you Cicades, chirp not so lowd sweet Birds
least you should wake my loue, thou gentle Banke

PLATE 5: FOL. 25b, LINES 1400–26 (HAND A)

HYMENS TRIVMPH

Giuen to the Colledge of
King Iames in Edinb.
by
William Drummond.

0.1–6] title and inscription added by Drummond, with a small pen flourish beneath *William Drummond*. Four early shelf-marks, three of them cancelled, to the right and above the title; blotting in later ink over and around *HYMENS*; above the title, smudged out, the letters *MSS*

The Speakers. [Fol. 1b]

Thyrsis
Palæmon freind to *Thyrsis*
Clarindo. *Siluia* disguised, ye beloved of *Thyrsis*
supposed to haue ben slaine by wild Beasts
Cloris a Nimph whome *Clarindo* served, & in
Loue wth *Thyrsis*.
⸢*Phillis* in loue wth *Clarindo*.⸣
Montanus in loue wth *Phillis*
Lidia Nurss to *Phillis*
Dorcas } fforesters
Siluanus }
Medorus. ffather to *Siluia*
Charimus. ffather to *Thyrsis*.
Chorus.. of Shepheards. /

1–16] transcribed by Hand A 5 *haue*] head of *a* badly formed *Beasts*] *B* badly formed 7, 8, and 9 *wth*] *t* not crossed 8] interlined after transcription of 7 and 9

To the right Noble Ladie
the Ladie of Roxborough [FOL. 2a]

That this small peece was (noble Ladie) borne
To be among those rites w^{c} did adorne
Yo^{r} worthy Nuptialls, I reioyce, as one
who ever longu'd to have his wishes showne
In any thing that might yor hono^{r} sound,
for that great goodnes I have ever found.
And, Madame, this much, I would have yo^{w} know
That I must evermore confess to owe
All gratitude vnto yor Noblenes,
who always have bene readie to express
yor love to virtue, and to doo me grace
w^{t} all sincere proceeding, in yor place.
w^{c}, that the world from mee may vnderstand
Here, Madame I subscribe it w^{t} my hand

Samuel Danyel

17–33] transcribed by Daniel 18] written in darker ink, not unlike that used by Hand A for italic in Fol. 1b 25 *And*] *A* touched up 26 *evermore*] perhaps *ever more* *confess*] ^{1}*s* badly formed

[BLANK] [FOL. 2b]

Actus Prim'. Scen. 1.
Thyrsis. / Palemon.

So to be reaft of all the ioyes of lyfe
How is it possible Palæmon
should ever any more a thought retayne
of the least comfort vppon Earth agayne?
noe, I would hate this hart, y^{t} hath recived
So deepe a wound, if it would ever com̃e
To bee recur'd, or would p*er*mitt a roome
To let in any other thinge then grief.
Pal. But Thyrsis, yo^{w} must, tell mee what's the cause
Th. Thinke but what cause I haue, when having passd
The heates, the Coldes the trembling Agonies
of feares, and hopes, and all the strange assalts
of passion that a tender hart could feale
In the attempt, and pursuite of his love,
And then to bee vndon when all was donne
To perish in the haven after all
Those Ocean sufferings, and even then to haue
my hopefull nuptiall bed, trurnd to a grave.
Pal. Good Thyrsis by what meanes I pray the tell?
Th. Tell thee Palæmon? how can I tell it thee
And liue? dost thou not see these feilds haue lost
Their glorie since y^{t} tyme *Siluia* was lost:
Siluia that onely deckt, y^{t} onely made
Arcadia shyne. Siluia, who was (ah woo the while
so miserably rent from off the world;
so rapt a way, as that no signe of her,
No peece was leaft to tell vs by what meanes,
Safe onely this poore remnant of her vayle,
All torne, and this deare lock of her rent hayre,
(W^{c} holy relicq*ue*s here I keepe w^{t} mee
The sad memorialls of her dismall fate)
Who sure deuour'd was vppon the shore
By ravinous beasts as she was walking there

Fol. 3a] numbered *2* in top right-hand corner 34–451] transcribed by Hand A 34 *Scen*] lower half of *S* not formed; letter resembles (perhaps written as) *C* 36 *Palæmon*] for *Palæmon, I* 40 *noe*] *oe* resembles *æ* 44 *mee*] ink blot above *m* *what's*] *s* written over indecipherable letter, perhaps a comma 53 *trurnd*] for *tournd* 55 *Palæmon?*] *?* written over comma 59 *while*] for *while)* 60 *world*] *r* added above *o* 62 *peece*] ^{2}*e* written over *r*; perhaps intended as *a* 68 *there*] ink blot above *re*

Alone it seemes, p*er*happs in seeking mee [Fol. 3b]
Or els retyr'd to meditate a part
The story of o^{r} loves, and heavy smart.
Pal. This is no newes yo^{w} tell of Siluias death:
That was long Since, why should yo^{w} wayle her now?
Th. Long since Palæmon, thinke yo^{w} any length
of tyme, can ever haue a power to make
A hart of flesh not morne, not griue, not pine,
That knowes, that feales that thinkes as much as myne?
Pal. But Thyrsis yo^{w} know how her father ment
To match her w^{t} Alexis, and a day
To celebrate the nuptialls was p^{r}fixt.
Th. True, he had such a purpose, but in vayne,
As, ô it was best knowne vnto vs twayne,
And hence it grew, that gaue vs both o^{r} feares.
That made our meeting stealth, o^{r} parting teares;
Hence was it y^{t}, w^{t} many'a secret wile
we robb'd o^{r} lookes, th'on-lookers to beguile,
This was the cause, ô miserable cause,
That made her by her selfe to stray alone;
w[c]^{ch} els, god knowes, she never should haue donne:
for, had o^{r} libertie as open ben
As were o^{r} loves, Siluia had not bene seene
w^{t}out her Thyrsis, never had we gone
But hand in hand, nor ever had mischaunce
Tooke vs asunder, she had all ways had
my bodie interposd betwixt all harmes
And her, but ah we had o^{r} libertie
Layd fast in prison when o^{r} loves were free.
Pal. But how know'st thou her love was such to thee?
Th. How doo I know the sun, the day from night?
Pal. weomens affections do like flashis prove,

69 *Alone*] left half of *o* heavily inked 84 *stealth,*] comma is continuation of tail of *h* 89 *w[c]ch*] *c* partly scratched out, *ch* written above, but unclear because the ink has spread on the damaged paper 91 *loves*] bottom of *v* heavily inked 99 *night?*] ? written above stop

They oft shew passion when they feale small love [Fol. 4a]
Th. Ah do not so profane that precious sex,
W^{c} I must ever reverence for her sake,
who was the glorie of her kinde, whose hart
In all her actions so transparent was,
As I might see it cleene and wholy myne.
Allwayes obseruing truth in one right lyne:
   How oft hath she bene vrg'd by fathers threats,
By frinds p*er*swasions, and Alexis sighes,
And teares, and prayears, to admitt his loue,
yet never could be wonne? How oft haue I
Beheld the bravest herds-men of theas playnes
(As what braue herds.men was then in the playns
of all Arcadia, that had not his hart
warm'd w^{t} her beames) to seeke to win her loue,
Ah I remember well, (and how can I
But evermore remember well?) when first
Our flame began, when scarse we knew what was
The flame we felt, when as we sate, and sigh'd,
And look'd vppon Each other and conciv'd
not what we ayld, yet something we did ayle,
And yet were well, and yet we were not well.
And what was o^{r} disease we could not tell;
Then would we kiss, then sight, then looke: and thus
In that first garden of o^{r} simplenes
We spent o^{r} childhood: but when yeares began
To ripe the frute of knowledg, ah how then,
Would she w^{t} graver lookes, w^{t} sweet-stern brow
Check my p^{r}sumption and my forwardnes;
Yet still would giue me flowres, still would she shew
What she would haue me, yet not haue me know

113 *herds.men*] perhaps *herds-men* 114 *of*] stain around *o* from ink blot on Fol. 4b (146 *co⟨.⟩ntends*) 118 *began*] *b* written over *w* (?false start for *when* following) 119 *The*] *h* written over indecipherable letter 120 *conciv'd*] *i* not dotted 124 *sight*] for *sigh*; *t* written over tail of *h* 127 *ripe*] *e* written over indecipherable letter (scratched out, causing damage to paper) 128 *sweet-stern*] hyphen written over comma

[FOL. 4b]

Pal. Alas w^{t} what pore coyne are lovers pay'd,
And taken w^{t} the smallest bayt is layd.
Th. And when in sportes w^{t} other company
of nimphs and Shephards we haue met abrode,
How would she steale a looke, and watch myne eye,
w^{c} way it went, and when at barly-breake
It came vnto my turne to reskue-her,
w^{t} what an earnest, swift, and nimble pace
would her affection make her feet to run,
And farther run then to my hand; her race
Had no stop but my bosome where to end.
And when we were to breake agayne, how late,
And loath her trimbling hand would part w^{t} myne,
And w^{t} how slow a pace would she set forth
To meete th'incountring party who co⟨.⟩ntends
T'attayne her, scarse affording him her fingers ends.
Pal. ffy Thyrsis w^{t} what fond remembrances
dost thou theas idle passions intertayne?
for shame leave off to wast yor youth in vayne,
And feed on shadowes. make yo^{wr} choyce anew,
Yo$^{[r]}$ other nimphs shall finde no doubt wilbe
As louely, and as fayre, and sweet, as she
Th. As fayre, and sweet as she? Palæmon peace,
Ah what can pictures be vnto the life?
what sweetnes can be found in Images?
w^{c} all nimphs els beside her, seeme to mee
she onely was a reall creature; she,
whose memorie must take vp all of mee.
should I another love, then must I have
Another hart, for this is full of her,
And evermore shalbe, here is she drawne
At length and whole; and more. this table is
A storie, and is all of her. and all
wrought in the liueliest coullors of my bloud,
And can there be a roome for others here?
should I disfigure such a peece, and blot

146 *co⟨.⟩ntends*] *o* and *n* heavily inked, ink blot between them obscures a letter; the scribe's attempts at correction above the blot have damaged the paper 151 *choyce*] *o* filled with ink 152 *Yo$^{[r]}$*] raised *r* struck through, presumably to indicate *Yow* is intended *doubt*] *b* heavily inked 155 *life?*] head of *?* written above a comma 165 *the*] head of *h* blotted

The p*er*fect'st workman-ship love ever wrought? [FOL. 5a]
Palæmon no, ah no, it cost to deare,
It must remayne intire whilst life remaynes,
The monument of her, and of my paynes

Pal. Thou mayst be such a fond Idolater
To dy for loue, though y^{t} were very strange,
Loue hath few Saints but many confessors,
And tyme no doubt will raze out all these notes
And leave a roome at length for other thoughts.

Th. yes, when there is no spring, no tree, no grove
In all Arcadia to record o^{r} loue.
And tell mee where we were (the tyme we were)
How we did walk together, what we sayd,
where we did ioy, and where we sate dismay'd.
And then I may farget her, not before;
Till then I must remember one so deare,
when every thing I see tells me of her
And yo^{w} deare Reliq*ue*s of y^{t} martir'd Saint
my hart adores, yo^{w}, the perpetuall bookes
whereon when teares p*er*mitt, myne eye still lookes,
Ah, yo^{w} were w^{t} her last, and till my last
yo^{w} must remayne w^{t} mee, yo^{w} were resserv'ed
To tell me she was lost, but yet alas
yo^{w} cannot tell mee how. I would yo^{w} could:
whits spotles vayle, cleene like her womandhood,,
w^{c} whilom covred the most lovely face,
That ever eye beheld, was there no messedg sent
from her by thee? ah yes there seemes it was,
Here is a T. made w^{t} her bloud, as yf
she would haue writen, Thyrsis I ame slayne
In seekinge thee, sure so it should haue bene,
And so I read it, and shall ever so.
And thou sweet remnant of the fayrest hayre
That ever wav'd w^{t} winde, ah thee I found
when her I hop'd to find, wrapt in a round
like to an O. the Character of woo;
As yf to say, O, Thyrsis I dy thyne

173 *y^{t}*] *y* written over *i* 175 *notes*] second downstroke of *n* not fully inked 182 *farget*] *o* written as *a* 187 *eye still*] space between these, for a two or three-letter word (nothing more in 1615) 192 *whits*] for *white* 196 *Here*] ^{2}*e* blotted 202 *wrapt*] *ra* altered, ?from other letters

This much yo^{w} tell me; yet dombe messengers [Fol. 5b]
of her last mynde, and what yo^{w} cannot tell
That I must thinke, w^{c} is the most extreeme
of wofullnes yt any hart can thinke.
Pal. There is no dealing w^{t} this man I see,
This humor must be let to spende it selfe
Vnto a lesser substance, ere y^{t} wee
Can any way apply a remedie.
But I lament his case, and so I know
doe all yt see him in this wofull plight,
And therefore will I leave him to him selfe,
for sorow y^{t} is full, hates others sight.
Th. Come boy whilst I contemplate these remaynes
of my lost loue vnder this mirtle tree
Record the dolefullst song, the sighing'st notes,
That musiq*ue* hath to intertayne sadd thoughts,
Let it be all at flatts, my, boy, all grave,
The tone that best befitts the griefe I haue.

So boy, now leaue me to my selfe that I
may be alone to grief, intire to misery.

Scen.2. [I. ii]

Cloris. Clarindo

Now gentle boy Clarindo, hast thou brought
my flocks into the feild? Cla. mistris I haue.
Clo. And hast thou told them? Cla. Yes
Clo. And are there all? Cla. All.
Clo. And hast thou leaft them safe my boy? Cla. safe
Clo. Then whilst they feede Clarindo, I must vse
thy service in a secret busynes,
But thow must doe it well my boy. Cla. the best I can.
Clo. dost thou know Thyrsis. Cla. yes
Clo. But know'st him well?
Cla. I haue good reason to know Thyrsis well.
Clo. what reason boy? Cla. I oft haue bene w^{t} him.
Clo. why then he knowes thee too.
Cla. yes I suppose, vnlesse he hath forgotten me of late

*209 *see,*] comma smudged, probably in another ink 222–3] space between these for two lines (1615 has fourteen) 224 *may*] *a* interlined above *my* 230 *And are*] space between these for one or two-letter word (nothing more in 1615) 231 *boy?*] *?* is tail of *y*, with no point 238 *boy?*] *?* made with two heads, but one point

Clo. But hath he heard thee sing my boy. Cla. he hath. [Fol. 6a]
Clo. Then doubtles he doth well remember thee.
Well, vnto him thou must a message doe
from thy sad mistries Cloris, but thou must
do it Exactly well, w^{t} thy best grace,
Best choyce of language, and best [g] Countenance.
I know thou canst doo well, and hast a speach.
And fashion pleasing to p*er*forme the same,
nor can I haue a fitter messenger
In this imployment, then thy self, my boy.
for sure, methinkes, noting thy forme and grace
That thou hast much of Siluia in thy face,
w^{c} yf he shall p*er*ceiue as well as I,
sure he will giue thee Audience willingly,
And for her sake, yf not for myne, heare out
Thy message, for he still, though she be dead,
Holdes sparkles of her vnextinguished,
And that is death to me, for though somtimes
Siluia and I most deare companions were,
yet when I saw he did so much p^{r}fer
Her before mee, I deadly hated her.
And was not sory for her death, and yet
was sory she should come to such a death,
But to the porpose, go to Thyrsis, boy,
say thou art Cloris servant sent to bee
The messinger of her distressed tears,
who languishes for him, and never shall
Haue comfort more, vnles he giue it her
Cla. I will. Clo. nay but stay boy, theris Somthinge els.
Tell him his cruelties makes me vndoo
my modestie, and to put on that part
w^{c} appertaynes to him, that is to woo,
And to disgrace my sex to shew my hart,
w^{c} no man els could haue had power to doo,
And that vnles he doo restore me back
Vnto my self, by his like love to me
I cannot liue, Cla. All this Ile tell him too.
Clo. Nay but stay boy, there is yet more,

246 *[g]*] scratched out, but still visible (eyeslip from 245 *grace*); head of *g* not finished 247 *hast*] *h* slightly blotted, ink marks above 250 *my*] small ink smudges above and below *m* 259 *companions*] first minim dotted in I*n* 265 *say*] head of *s* not properly formed, or not inked fully

Tell him, it will no hono^{r}, be to him [Fol. 6b]
When ever it shall come to be made knowne,
That he hath ben her death w^{c} was his owne,
And how his loue hath fatall bene to twoe
distressed nimphs. Cla this will I tell him too.
Clo. Nay but stay boy, wilt thou say nothinge els
As of thy selfe, to waken vp his love?
Thou mayst say somthing, w^{c} I may not say,
And tell him, how thou holdst me full as fayre,
Yea and more fayre, more lovily, more compleate
Then ever Siluia was, more wise, more stayd,
How she was but a light and waveringe mayd
Cla. Nay there I leave yo^{w} that I cannot saye.
Clo. what sayst thou boy? Cla. nothinge but y^{t} I will
Endevo^{r} all I can to worke his love,
Clo. doo good my boy, but thou must yet add more
As from thy self, and say what an vnkinde,
And barbarous parte it is to suffer thus
so bewtious and rare a nimph to pyne,
And perish for his love, and such a one
As yf she would have stoop'd to others flame
hath had the gallantst herdsmen of theies feildes
fall at her feete, all wch she[th] hath dispised
having her hart before by thee surprisd
and now doth nothing els but sit & morne;
Speak Thyrsis, weepe Thyrsis, sigh Thyrsis, and
sleepe Thyrsis when she sleepes, wch is but rare,
Besides good Boy thou must not stick to sweare
thow oft hast seene me sowne, & sincke to grownd
in, theis deepe passions wherein I abound,
for somthing thou maist say beyond the truth
by reason of my loue, & of thie youth,
do good Clarindo sweare, & vow thus much
    But dost thou now remember all I sayd?
dost thou forget no p*ar*cell of my speach?

287] ink dot to the left, in line with punctuation in speech-prefixes at 284 and 291 288 *lovily*] *i* not dotted *compleate*] *m* touched up 291 *saye*] mishapen *y* resembles *x* 301 *she[th]* the scribe wrote *shath*, then scratched out *th* and altered *a* to *e* *dispised*] ^{2}*s* written over *t* 303 *els*] raised slightly above the line

shall I repeat [no] the same againe to thee? [Fol. 7a]
or els wilt thou rehearce it vnto me?
that I may know thou hast it p*er*fect, Boy?

Cla. No, that needes not, be sure I will report
what yow inioyne me in most earnest sorte.

Clo. Ah doo good Boy, although I feare it will
availe me little, for I doubt his hart
is repossessed wth an other loue.

Cla. Another loue, whoe may that bee I pray?

Clo. wth Amarillis. I haue heard, for they
are thought will in the end, make vp a match.

Cla. wth Amarillis? well, yet will I go,
and trie hies humor whether it be so.

Clo. Goe good Clarendo, but thou must not faile
to worke effectually for my availe,
And doe not stay, retorne wth speed good Boy.
my passions are to great, t'indure delay

Act.2. *Scen. 3.* [I. iii]

Clarindo. Sol.

Thyrsis in loue with *Amarillis?* then
in what case ame I? what doth availe
this altred habit that belyes my *sex?*
what bootes t'haue estap't from Pyrats hands,
and wth such wiles to haue deceiued *their wills,*
if I returne to fall on worser ills?
In loue wth Amarillis? is that so?
Is Siluia then forgot that hath indur'd
so much for him? doo all theis miseries
caused by his meanes, deserue no better hire?
was it the greatest comfort of my life

314 *shall*] *a* altered from *e* *[no]*] scratched out (?eyeslip from 313 *no*) *321 *repossessed*] the scribe wrote *repossed*; another hand struck out *d* and interlined *ssed* in italic above the deletion, with two carets 326–7] space between these for one line (1615 has no extra line) 327 *Goe*] *e* only half formed *Clarendo*] *e* dotted 331 *2*] for *1* *335 *sex?*] added in italic hand 336 *estap't*] for *escap't* *337 *their wills,*] added in italic hand 338–9] half-line space between these lines 340 *indur'd*] written as *in dur'd*, with ²*d* over *s*

to haue return'd that I might comfort him, [Fol. 7b]
And ame I welcom'd thus? ah did mine eyes
take never rest after I was ariu'd
till I had seen him, though vnknown to him?
being hidden thus, & cou'red wth disguise
and masculine attyre to *temporize*
vntill Alexis mariadge day be past,
wch shortly as I heare, will be: and w^{ch}
would free me wholly from my ffatheres feare,
whoe if hee knew I were return'd, would yet
vndoo I doubt that Match, to matc'h me there,
wch would be more then all my suffrings were
    Indeed me thought when I beheld the face
of my deare Thyrsis, I beheld a face
confounded all wth passion, wch did much
afflict my hart, but yet I little thought
It could haue ben for any others loue;
I did svppose the memory of mee,
and of my rapture had possest him so,
as made him shew that contenance of wo,
and much adoe had I then to forbeare
from casting me into his Arms, & yeald
What comfort my poore selfe could yeald, but y^{t}
I thought o^{r} ioyes would not haue ben compleat
but might haue yelded vs annoyes as great,
vnlesse I could come wholy his, & cleer'd
from all those former daugeres wch wee feard.
wch now a little stay (though any stay
be death to me) would wholy take away;
    And therefore I resolu'd my self to beare
this burthen of o^{r} suffrings yet a while
And to become a Servant in this guise
to her I would haue skorned other wise.

*349 *temporize*] added in italic hand   350 *Alexis*] *x* resembles *y*   351] ink point to the left   *heare*] ^{1}*e* altered from *a*   354 *mat'ch*] *t* and *c* fused (letter resembles *k*)   355–6] half-line space between these lines   356 *the*] *e* written over *y*, scratched out   361 *svppose*] *v* squeezed in between *s* and ^{1}*p*   363 *that*] *t* written over *w*   366 *yeald*] *y* altered from *g*   370 *daugeres*] for *dangeres* or *daũgeres* (1615: *dangers*)   *feard*] *e* altered from *r*   372 *me)*] bracket written over high, large comma, or an earlier attempt at a bracket   376 *wise*] upper loop of *s* blotted

and be at all Com̃aunds to go and come, [FOL. 8a]
to trudge into the feilds early & late,
wch though I know, it misbecomes my state,
yet it becomes my fortune, w^{c} is that,
not Phillis whome I serue, but since I serue,
I will do what I doo most faithefully..
But Thyrsis is it possible that thow
shouldest so forget me, & forgoe thie vow?
Or is it but a flying vaine report
that slanders thy affec͠con in this sorte?
It may be so, & God graunt it be so.
I shall soone finde if thou be false or no;
but ah heere comes my fury. I muest fly

Act.2. *Scen. 4.* [I. iv]
Phillis. Clarindo.

Ph. Ah cruell youth whether away so fast?
Cla. Good Phillis doe not stay me, I haue haste.
Ph. What haste shouldst thou haue but to comfort mee?
Whoe hath noe other comfort but in thee?
Cla. Alas thou dost but troble me in vaine,
I cannot help thee, t'i[c]s not in my power.
Ph. Not in thy powre Clarindo? ah if thou
hadst any thing of manlines, thou wouldst.
Cla. But if I haue not, what doth it availe
in this sort to torment thy self & mee?
And therefore prithee *Phillys* let me go.
Ph. Ah whether canst thou go, where thou shalt be
more dearlie lou'd & cheerisht then wth me?
Cla. But that my purpose cannot satisfie,
I must be gone, there is no remedye
Ph. O cruell youth will thy hart nothing mooue
shew me yet pittie, if thou shew not loue

380 *becomes*] *m* and *e* fused *fortune*] *o* altered from *a* 385] ink point just before start of line 387 ^{2}*be so*] written as one word 388 *no*] small ink blot above *n* 390 *2*] for *1* *392 *Ph.*] added in italic hand *393 *haste*] *e* perhaps added by another hand *394 *haste*] *e* added by the hand which added 392 *Ph.* 400 *Cla. But*] short horizontal stroke between these words 401 *mee?*] point of *?* is a comma

Cla. Beleeue me *Phillis* I doe pitty thee, [Fol. 8b]
and more, lament thy error; so fare well.
Ph. And art thou gon hard-harted youth? hast thou
thus disappainted my desires, & least
my shame t'afflict me worser then my love?
Now in what case am I, that neither can
recall my modestie, nor thee againe?
Ah were it now to doe againe, my passions should
haue smothred me to death, before I would
haue [she]wed the smallest sparckle of my flame,
But it is doñe, & I ame now vndon.
Ah hadst thou ben a man, & had that part
of vnderstanding of a womans hart
my words had ben vnborne, only mine eyes
had ben a tongue enough to one were wise,
But this it is to loue a Boy, whose years
conceaues not his owne good, nor weighes my teares,
but this disgrace I iustlie haue deseru'd

Scen .5. [I. v]
Lidia. Phillis

Lid. So *Phillis*, haue yo^{w}, and y'are rightly seru'd.
haue yo^{w} disdayn'd the gallanst fforresters
And brauest Herdsmen all *Arcadia* hath?
and now in loue wth one is not a man?
Assure yor self this is a iust revenge
loue takes for ⌜*your*⌝ misprision of [ther] ⌜*his*⌝ powre.
I tould yo^{w} often there would come a time
when yo^{w} would [laugh] sure be plaug'd for such a cryme,
but yo^{w} would laugh at me as one yo^{w} thought
conceiu'd not of what mettaile yo^{w} were wrought
Is this yo^{w} whoe would wonder any Nimph
could ever be so foolish as to loue?

409 *Phillis*] loops of *ll* blotted 412 *disappainted*] ^{2}*a* for *o* *least*] long *s* has horizontal stroke, perhaps to indicate *f* 413 *me*] *e* written over *y*, scratched out badly 414 *neither*] ^{1}*e* altered from *i* 416] ink blot to left, in margin 418 *[she]wed*] *she* deleted with horizontal stroke (1615: *shew'd*) 419 *it*] *t* altered from *s* 423 *enough to*] pen not taken off between *h* and *t* 426 *disgrace*] *g* altered from *r* 431 *brauest*] ink blot below *u* *434 *your*] interlined in italic hand, above a caret, between *for* and *misprision* *his*] interlined in italic hand, above deletion of *ther*, with a caret 436 *[laugh]*] deleted with single horizontal stroke (eyeslip for 437 *laugh*)

who is so foolish now? *Ph.* peace *Lidia* peace [Fol. 9a]
Add not more greif t'a hart that hath to much,
do not insult vpon her miserye
whose flame, God wote, needes water & not oyle.
  Thou seest I ame vndon, caught in the toyle
of an intangling mischeif, tell me how
I may recover, and vnwinde me now.
Lid. That doth require more time, wee will [apast] *aparte*
consult thereof, be yo^w but rul'd by mee.
and yo^w shall finde, I yet [will] ⌜*I'le*⌝ set yo^w free.

Exeunt.

The Song of the first Chorus.

Love is a sicknes full of woes
All remedies refusing
A plant that w^t most cutting growes
most barrayne w^t best vsing
Why so
more we inioy it more it dyes
yf not inioyd it sighing cryes
Hey ho. |

447 *recover*] *c* blotted *448 *aparte*] added in italic hand after deletion of *apast* *450 *I'le*] interlined in italic hand above deletion of *will*, with a caret (1615: *I, yet, will*) 452–68] transcribed by Daniel 454 *remedies*] *i* touched up 458 ²*more*] *m* ?blotted 459 *sighing*] ¹*i* not dotted

Love is a torment of the mynde [Fol. 9b]
A tempest ever lasting
And Iove hath made it of that kinde
nor well nor full nor fasting
why so
more we inioy it, more it dyes
yf not inioyd it, sighing cryes
Hey ho.

466 *we*] three marks at the head of the first stroke of *w* ink, or made with a sharpened nib

*466 and *467 *it,*] commas added in darker

Actus. Secu: Scæn. 1.
Siluanus. Dorcas. Montanus.

In what a meane regard are wee now held
Wee actyue and laborious forresters,
(Who though o^{r} living rurall [were] ⌜*bee*⌝, and rough)
Yet heretofore were wee for vallo^{r} priz'd,
And well esteemd in all good companies.
Nor would the dayntiest nymphes that valleys haunt
or feilds inhabite, euer haue dispizd
Our siluane songs, nor yet our playne discourse.
But gracefully accepted of our skill
And often of our loues, when they haue seene
How faithfull and how constant we haue bene.

Dor. Its true *Siluanus*, but you see the tymes
Are altred now, and they soe dainty growne
By beeing ador'd, and woo'd, and followed so
of those vnsynued amourous heardsmen, who
By reason of their rich and mightie flocks
Supplie their pleasures wth that plenteousnes
As they disdaine our playnenes, and doo skorne
our companie, as men rude and ill borne.

Sil: Well so they doo. but *Dorcas* if you marke
How oft they doe miscarrie in their loue,
And how disloyall theis fine heardsmen proue,
you shall perceiue how their aboundant store
Payes not their expectation, nor desires,
Witnes theis groues wherin they oft deplore
The miserable passions they sustaine,
And how perfidious, wayward, and vnkinde
They finde their loues to be. wch wee who are
The .

Fol. 10a] numbered *3* in top right-hand corner 469–1229] transcribed by Hand B *473 *(Who ... rough)*] brackets added by another hand, in the same colour of lighter brown ink used by Daniel on Fol. 9b; the same ink was used for the other alterations in 473–4 *bee,*] interlined in italic hand above deletion of *were* (cancelled with a single horizontal stroke), with a caret; the same hand added the comma after the deletion *474 *priz'd,*] comma added by another hand 491 *doe*] *e* blotted *491 *loue,* *492 *proue,* *494 *desires,* *496 *sustaine,*] commas added in lighter brown ink 493 *shall*] *a* not properly formed

The eyes and eares of woods, oft see and heare; [Fol. 10b]
ffor hether to theis groues they much resorte,
And here one wayles a part the vsage hard
of her disordered, wilde, and wilfull mate:
There mournes another her vnhappie state
As held restraynd, and euer in suspect.
Another to her trustie confident
Laments how shee is matcht to such a one
As cannot giue a woman her content.
Another greiues how shee hath got a foole
Whose bed, although she loath, shee must indure.
And thus they all vnhappie by that meanes
W^{ch} they account would bring all happines,
most wealthely are plagu'd wth rich distresse.

Dor. And so they are, but yet this was not wont
To be the fashion heere, there was a tyme
Before *Arcadia* came to be diseas'd
Wth theis corrupted humors raigning now
That choice was made of virtue and deseart
Wthout respect of any other ends.
When Loue was only maister of their harts
And rul'd alone, when simple thoughts produc'd
Playne honest deedes, and eueryone contends
To haue his fame to follow his desearts
And not his shewes, to be the same he was,
Not seem'd to be. and then were no such parts
of false deceiuings playd, as now wee see.
But after that accursed greedynes
of wealth began to enter and possesse
The harts of men, integritie was lost,
And wth it they themselues. for never more
Came they to be in their owne powre againe
That

*499 *heare;*] comma added in lighter brown ink below stop, to make a semicolon *500 *resorte,* *511 *happines,* *528 *lost,*] commas added in lighter brown ink 506 *Laments*] mark above *s* 508 *foole*] continuation of *e* looks like a comma 529 *never more*] words are linked

That Tyrant vanquisht them, made them all slaues, [FOL. 11a]
That brought base seruitude into the world,
wch els had neuer bene. that onely made
Them to indure all whatsoeuer waights
Powre could devise to lay vpon their necks;
ffor rather then they would not haue; they would not bee
But miserable. so that no deuise
Needes ells to keepe them vnder; they themselues
will beare farr more, then they are made, themselues
will add vnto their fetters, rather then
They would not be, or held to be, rich men.

Sil. Then *Dorcas*, how, much more are wee to prize
our meane estate, wch they so much dispise?
Considring that wee doo enioy thereby
The dearest thing in nature, libertie:
And are not tortur'd wth those hopes and feares
Th'affliction layd on superfluities,
wch make them to obserue, and serue the tymes;
But are content wth what the earth, the woods,
And Rivers nere doo readily afforde.
And therewthall furnish our homely bourd.
Those vnbought Cates please our vnlearned throats
That vnderstand not daynties, euen as well
As all their delycates, wch doe but stuffe
And not sustaine the stomacke; and indeed
A well obeying belly doth make much
ffor libertie. for hee that doth but live
Although wth Rootes, and haue no hopes, is free
wthout the verge of any sourayntie.
And is a Lord at home, Comaunds the day
As his till night, and then reposes him
Att his owne howres. thinks on no stratagem
But how to take his game. hath no diseigne
To crosse next day. No plotts to vndermyne.

But

*531 *slaues,*] ?comma added *532 *world,*] comma added in lighter brown ink 534 *indure*] *e* blotted *waights*] *ai* interlined above caret, written over ?*i* 541 *held*] ?*e* altered 548 *tymes*] *s* blotted 551 *therewthall*] *er* touched up *bourd*] *d* ends with downstroke which may signify *s*

Dor. But whie *Montanus* doo you looke so sad, [Fol. 11b]
What is the cause your minde is not as free
As yor estate? what haue you had of late
Some coy repulse of your disdainefull nymph
To whome loue hath subdu'de you? who indeed
our onely master is, and no Lord els
But hee, hath any powre to vex vs here,
wch had hee not, wee too too happie were.

Mon. In troth I must confesse, when now you twoe
found me in yonder thickett, I had lost
my self, by having seene that wch I would
I had not had theis eyes to see. and iudge
Yf I great reason haue not to, complayne.
You see I am a man, though not so gay
And delycately cladd, as are your fine
And amourous dayntie herdsmen. yet a man,
And that not base, not vnally'de to *Pan*.
And of a spirite doth not degenerate
from my Robustious manly ancestors.
Being neuer foyld in any wrastling game
But still haue borne away the cheifest prize
In euery braue and actyue exercise;
Yet not wthstanding, that disdainefull maide
Prowd *Phillis* doth dispise me and my loue,
And will not daigne so much as heare me speake
But doth abiure forsooth the thought of loue.
Yett shall I tell you? (yet asham'd to tell
This coy vnloving soule, I saw ere while
Solicyting a youth, a smooth fac'd boy,
whome in her armes shee held (as seemd to me,
Being closely busht a pretty distance off)
Against his will. and wth strange passion vrg'd his.

*565 *sad,*] comma added in lighter brown ink 568 *disdainefull*] ^{2}*i* not dotted *569 *you?*] ?head of question mark added 581 *vnally'de*] head of *y* blotted 591 *tell*] for *tell)*

his stay. who seem'd, struggled to gett away [FOL. 12a]
And yet shee stayd him, yet, intreats his stay
Att wch strange sight, imagine I that stood
Spectator, how confoundedly I stood
And hardly could forbeare from running in,
To clayme for myne, if euer loue had right
Those her imbraces cast away in sight
But staying to behould the end, I stayd
Too long, the boy getts loose, her self retyres,
And you came in; but if I live, that boy
shall deerely pay for his misfortune, that
Hee was belou'd of her of whome I would
Haue none on earth beloued, but my self.

Dor. That were to byte the stone, a thing vniust
To punish him for her conceiued lust.

Mon. Tush many in this world we see are caught
And suffer for misfortune, not their fault.

Sil. But that would not become yor manlynes
Montanus, it were shame for valiant men
To doo vnworthilie.

Mon. Speake not of that *Siluanus*, if my rage
Irregular be made, it must worke like effects

Dor. Theis are but billowes, tombling after stormes
They last not long, come lett some exercise
divert that humor, and convert your thoughts
To know your self. skorne her who skorneth you,
Idolatrize not so that sex. but hold
A man of Straw, more then a wife of gold. /

Exeunt. /

Fol. 12a] numbered *4* (head cropped) in top right-hand corner
621 *convert*] *e* blotted
624–5] pen flourish between these lines

Actus.2. Scæn.2. [II. ii] [Fol. 12b]

Lidia. Phillis. |

You must not *Phillis* be so sensible
of theis small touches wch your passion makes.
Phi. Small touches *Lidia*? doo you count them small?
Can there vnto a woman worse befall?
Then hath to me? what, haue not I lost all
That is most deere to vs, loue, and my fame?
Is there a third thing *Lidia* you can name?
That is so pretious as to match wth theis?
Lid. Now sealy girle, how fondly doo you talke,
How haue you lost your fame? what for a few
Ill favord foolish wordes vttred in ieast
vnto a foolishe youth? Cannot you say
You did but to make triall how you could
if such a peevishe qualme of passion should
(as never shall) oppresse your tender hart,
fframe yor conceipt to speake, to looke, to sigh,
like to a hart strooke lover. and that you
perceiuing him to be a bashfull youth
Thought to put spirit in him, and make you sport.
Phi. Ah *Lidia*, but he saw I did not sporte
Hee saw my teares, and more, what shall I say?
He saw too much, and that, wch never man
Shall euer see againe, whilst I haue breath.
Lid. Are you so simple as you make your self, ?
What did hee see? a counterfeited shew
of passion, wch you may, if you were wise
make him as easilie to vnbeleiue
As what he never saw. and thinke his eyes
Conspir'd his vnderstanding to deceiue.
How many women thinke you, being espide
In neerer touching cases, by mischance,
Haue yet not only fac'd their lovers downe
ffor what they saw; and brought them to beleiue
They

631 *befall?*] point of *?* is a comma

[FOL. 13a]

They had not seene the thing wch they had seene,
Yea and to sweare it too. and to condempne
Themselues. such meanes can witt devise,
To make mens myndes vncredite their owne eyes.
And therefore lett not such a toy as this
disease your thoughts. and for your losse of loue
It is as much as nothing. I would turne
A passion vpon that, should overturne
It cleane. and that is wrath, one heate
Expells another. I would make my thoughts of skorne
To be in heigth so much aboue my loue
As they should ease and pleasure more by farr.
I would disdayne to cast a looke that way
Where hee should stand, vnles it were in skorne
Or thinke a thought of him, but how to worke
Him all disgrace that possiblie I could.

Phi. That *Lidia* can I never doo. lett him
doo what hee will to mee. report my shame
And vaunt his fortune, and my weaknes blame.

Lid. Nay as for that he shalbe so well charm'd
ere I haue done, as you shall feare no tales.

Phi. Ah *Lidia* could that be, wthout his harme
How blesste should I bee. but see where comes
my great tormentor that rude fforrester,
Good *Lidia* lett vs fly, I hate his sight
Next to the ill I suffer: Lett vs fly,
Wee shall be troubled wth him woefully.

Lid. Content you *Phillis*, stay and heare him speake
Wee may make vse of him more then you thinke.

Phi. what vse can of so grosse a peece be made?

Lid. The better vse be sure, for being grosse
Your subtler spirits full of their fynesses
serve their owne turnes in others busynesses

what

685 *his*] perhaps written as *this*   693] pen flourish between this line and the catchword

Actus. 2. Scæn. 3. [II. iii] [FOL. 13b]

Montanus, Lidia. Phillis. |

What pleasure can I take to chace wilde beasts
when I my self am chac'd more egarly
By myne owne passions, and can finde no rest?
Lett them who haue their harts at libertie
Attend those sports. I cannot be from hence
Where I receiu'd my hurt, heere must I tread
The maze of my perplexed miserie.
And here see where shee is, the cause of all.
And now what shall I doo? what shall I say?
How shall I looke? how stand? wch vtter first?
my love or wrath? alas I know not w^{ch}.
Now were it not as good haue beene away
As thus to come, and not tell what to say?

Phi. See *Lidia* see, how savagely hee lookes
Good lett vs goe, I never shall indure
To heare him bellow. *Lidia*. prethee *Phillis* stay,
And giue him yet the hearing, in respect
Hee loues you. otherwise you shew yor self
A savage more then hee. *Phill*. well if I heare
I will not answere him a word, you shall replie
And prethee *Lidia* doo, replie for mee.

Lid. ffor that wee shall, *Phillis* doo well enough
when hee begyns, who seemes is very long
To giue the onsett. sure the man is much
Perplexed, or he studies what to say.

Phi. And *Lidia* see how hee hath trickt himself
Now sure this gay fresh suite, as seemes to mee
Hangs like greene yvie on a rotten tree.

Lid. Some beasts doo weare gray beards beside yor goats
And beare wth him, this suite bewrayes yong thoughts.

Mon. Ah was it not ynough to be opprest
Wth that confounding passion of my loue

And.

710 *indure*] ?*d* written over *e* 712 *yet*] *e* blotted *respect*] head of ^{2}*e* blotted

And her disdayne, but that I must be torne [Fol. 14a]
wth wrath and envye too ? and haue no vayne
free from the racke of suffring, that I can
Nor speake, nor thinke, but most distractedly. ?
How shall I now begyn that haue no way
To lett out any passion by it self
But that they all will thrust together so
As none wilbe expressed as they ought.
But something I must say now I am here,
And be it what it will, Loue, Envie, wrath,
or all together in a Comberment
my words must be like mee, perplext and rent.
And so Ile to her. *Phi. Lidia* see hee comes
Lid. Hee comes indeed, and as me thinks doth shew
more trouble in his face by farr then loue.
Mon. ffayre *Phillis*, and too fayre for such a one
vnles you kinder were, or better then
I know you are. how much I haue indur'd
for you, although you skorne to know, I feele.
And did imagine that in beeing a man,
who might deserue regard, I should haue been
Prefer'd before a boy. but well I see.
your seeming, and your being disagree.
Phi. What *Lidia* doth he brawle ? what meanes he thus
To speake, and looke in this strange sort on mee ?
Mon. Well modest *Phillis* neuer looke so coy,
Theis eyes beheld you dallying wth a boy.
Phi: Mee wth a boy *Montanus* ? when, where, how ?
Mon. Too day, heere,   and most laciviouslie
Lid. Ha ha, belike, hee saw you *Phillis* when
This morning you did stryue wth *Cloris* boy
To haue your garland wch he snatcht away
And kept it from you by strong force and might
And you againe laid hold vpon the same,
And held it fast, vntill wth much adooe,
hee.

Fol. 14a] numbered 5 in top right-hand corner 732 *way*] *a* touched up 756 *heere, and*] space between these for one or two words (1615: *here, in most*) 757 *when*] followed by mark, perhaps a pen rest 758 *wth*] *t* not crossed 762 *wth*] *t* not crossed

He wrong it from your hands, and gott away. [FOL. 14b]
And this is that great matter wch hee saw.
Now fy *Montanus* fy, are you so grosse
T'imagine such a worthie Nymphe as shee
would be in loue wth such a Youth as hee?
whie now you haue vndone your credite quite
You neuer can make her amends for this,
So impious a surmize. nor euer can
Shee, as shee reason hath, but must dispise
Your grossnes, who rather should haue come in
And righted her, then suffer such a one
To offer an indignitie so vile,
And you stand prying in a bush the while.

Mon. what doo I heare? what, am I not my self
how? haue myne eyes double vndone me then?
ffirst seing *Phillis* face, and now her fact,
or els the fact I saw, I did not see?
And sence thou hast my vnderstanding wrong'd
And traytor like given false intelligence
whereby my iudgment comes to passe amisse.
And yet I thinke my sence was in the right
And yet in this amaze I cannott tell
But howsoere, I in an errour am
In Loving or beleiving, or in both
And therefore *Phillis* at thy feet I fall
And pardon crave for this my grosse surmise. /

Lid But this *Montanus* will not now suffise
You quite haue lost her, and your hope and all.

Mon. Good *Lidia* yett intreate her to relent
And lett her but commaund me any thing
That is wthin the powre of man to doo,
And shee shall finde *Montanus* will performe
More then a Gyant, and will stead her more
Then all the heardsmen in *Arcadia* can.

Shee.

768 *you*] head of *y* blotted

Lid. She will comaund you nothing, but I wishe [FOL. 15a]
you would a litle terrifie that boy
for his presumption, and so charme his tongue
As hee may neuer dare to vse her name
But in all reverence as is fitt for her.
But doo not you examyne him a word
ffor that were neither for your dignitie
Nor hers, that such a boy as hee should stand
And iustifie himself in such a case.
who would but fayne vntruthes vnto yor face.
And herein you some service shall performe
As may perhapps make her to thinke on you.
Mon. Alas this is a worke so low, so farr
beneath my worth, as I esteeme it none,
were it t'incounter some feirce mountayne beast
or monster, it were something fitting mee.
But yet this will I doo, and doe it home
Assure you *Lidia*, as I live I will.
Phi. But yet I would not haue you hurt the youth
ffor that were neither grace for you nor mee,
Mon. That as my rage will tollerate, must bee. /

Actus.2. Scæn.4. [II. iv]

Cloris. Clarindo. /

Here comes my long-expected messenger
God graunt the newes he brings may make amends
for his long stay. and sure I hope it will.
Me thinks his face bewrayes more iollitie
In his returning, then in goeing hence
Cla. Well, all is well, no *Amarillis* hath
Supplanted *Siluias* loue in *Thirsis* hart.
Nor any shall. but see where *Cloris* lookes
ffor.

817–18] pen flourish between these lines

ffor what I shall not bring her at this tyme [Fol. 15b]

Clo. *Clarindo* though my longing would be faine
dispatch't at once, and heare my doome pronounc'd
All in a word of either life or death
Yett doo not tell it but but by circumstance.
Tell me the manner where, and how thou foundst
My *Thirsis*, what he said, how look'd, how far'd
How he receau'd my message, vsed thee,
And all in breife, but yet be sure tell all. /

Cla. All will I tell, as neere as I can tell,
ffirst after teadious searching vp and downe
I found him all alone like a hurt deare
Gott vnder Cover in a shadie grove,
Hard by a litle Christall purling spring
wch but one sullen note of murmer held
And where no sun could see him. where no eye
Might overlooke his lovely privacie.
There in a path of his owne making, trode
Bare as a comen way, yet lead no way
Beyond the turnes he made (wch were but short)
wth Armes acrosse, his hatt downe on his eyes
(As if those shades yelded not shade ynow
To darken them), hee walks wth often stopps
vneven pace, like motions to his thoughts.
And when he heard me coming. for his eares
were quicker watches then his eyes, it seem'd
Hee sudainely lookes vp, stayes sudainely,
And wth a brow that told how much the sight
of any interupter troubled him,
Beheld me, wthout speaking any word
As if expecting what I had to say.
I finding him in this confusd dismay
who heretofore had been farr otherwise
I must confesse, for tell you all I must
A trembling passion ouerwhelmd my brest
So that I likewise stood confusd, and dombe

And.

829 *faine*] horizontal stroke above *ne* 831 *either life*] words are linked 832 *but but*] for *but*
848 *Armes*] *A* written over *a* 862 *ouerwhelmd*] ^{1}*e* blotted

And onely look'd on him, as hee on mee. [FOL. 16a]
In this strange posture, like twoe statues wee
Remaynd a while, but wth this difference sett.
Hee blusht, and I look'd pale. my face did shew
Ioy to see him, his trouble to be seene.
At length bethinking me for what I came,
what part I had to act, I rowzd my spirits,
And sett my self to speake. although I wisht
Hee would haue first begun. and yet, before
A word would issue, twice I bowd my knee,
Twice kist my hand, my action so much was
more readie then my tongue. at last I told
whose messenger I was, and how I came
To intymate the sad distressed case
of an afflicted Nymphe, whose only help
Remaynd in him. Hee when he heard the name
of *Cloris*, turnes away his head and shrinks
As if he greev'd that you should greiue for him.
Clo: No no it troubled him to heare my name
wch he dispises, is he so perverse
And wayward still? ah then I see no hope.
Clarindo, would to god thou hadst not gone,
I could be but as now I am, vndonne.
Cla. Haue patience Mistres, and but heare the rest.
When I perceiu'd his suffring, wth the touch
And sudaine stop it gaue him, presently
I layd on all the waights that motion might
procure, and him besought, abiur'd, invok'd
By all the rights of nature, pietie,
And manlynes, to heare my message out.
Told him how much the matter did import
Yo^{r} saftie and his fame. how he was bound
In all humanitie to right the same.
Clo. That was well done my boy, what said he then?
Cla. Hee turnes about, and fixt his eyes on me
Content to giue his eares a quiet leave
To

865 *twoe*] first stroke of *w* written across the *t* 888 *perceiu'd*] ?*perceu'id* *wth*] *t* not crossed
889 *sudaine*] smudging around *d*

[Fol. 16b]

To heare me. when I fayld not to relate
All what I had in charge, and all he heares
And lookes directly on me all the while.
Clo: I doubt hee noated thee more then thy words.
But now *Clarindo*, what was his replie?
Cla. Thus. Tell faire *Cloris*, my good boy, how that
I am not so disnatured a man
Or so ill borne to disesteeme her loue
or not to greiue, as I protest I doo
That shee should so afflict herself for mee.
But. *Clo:* Ah now comes that bitter word of But
wch makes all nothing that was said before,
That smoothes and woundes, that stroakes & dashes more
Then flatt denialls, or a playne disgrace.
But tell me yet what followed on that But
Cla. Tell her said hee, that I desire shee would
Redeeme her self at any price shee could
And neuer lett her thinke on me, who am
But even the barke and outside of a man,
That trades not wth the living, neither can
Nor euer will keepe other company
Then wth the dead. my *Siluias* memorie
Is all that I must euer liue wthall.
wth that his teares, wch likewise forced myne
Sett me againe vpon another racke
of passion so, that of my self I sought
To comfort him the best I could devise
And I besought him that he would not be
Transported thus. But know that wth the dead
Hee should no more convers, and how his loue
was lyving, that would giue him all content
And was all his intyre, and pure, and wisht
To lyue no longer then shee should be soe.
When

913 *playne*] *p* and *y* written over indecipherable letters, neatly scratched out   923 *myne*] *y* resembles *g*

When more I would haue said, he shooke his head [FOL. 17a]
And willd me speake no further at that tyme
But leaue him to him self, and to returne
Againe anone, and hee would tell me more.
Comending me for having done the part
Both of a true and moving messenger.
And so I tooke my leaue, and came my way. /
Clo: Returne againe? no, to what end?
Yf hee be so conceipted and so fond
To enterteyne a shadow, I haue done,
And wish that I had neuer done so much.
Shall I discend below my self to send
To one is not himself? Lett him alone
wth his dead ymage; you shall go no more.
Haue I here fram'd wth all the art I could
This garland, deckt wth all the various flowres
Arcadia yeildes, in hope he would send backe
Some comfort, that I might therewth haue crown'd
His loue, and witness'd myne, in th'endles round
of this faire ring, the character of ffaith;
But now he shall haue none of it. I rather will
Rend it in peeces, and dishatter all
Into a Chaos, like his formeles thoughts.
But yet thou sayst he will'd thee to returne,
And he would tell thee more. *Cla.* yes so hee said.
Clo. Perhapps thy words might yet so worke wth him
As that hee takes this tyme to thinke on them.
And then I should doo wrong to kepe thee backe.
Well, thou shalt goe, and Carry him from mee
This garland, worke it what effect it will.
But yet I know it will doo nothing; stay
Thou shalt not goe, for sure he said but that
To

958 *wth*] *t* not crossed 960 *doo*] ^{2}*o* blotted

To put thee off, that hee might be alone. [Fol. 17b]
Att his Idolatrie, in worshipping
A nothing, but his self made ymages.
But yet he may be wearyed wth those thoughts
As having worne them long, and end they must.
And this my message coming in fitt tyme
And movingly deliuered, may take hold.
Hee said thou wert a moving messenger
Clarindo did hee not. *Cla*. yes so hee said.
Clo. Well thou shallt goe. And yet if any thought
of me should move him, hee knowes well my mynde
(if not too well) and where hee may me finde.
Tho shalt not goe *Clarindo*, nor will I
disgrace me more wth importunitie.
And yett if such a motion should take fire
And finde no matter readie, it would out.
And oportunities must not be slackt
Clarindo, thou shalt goe, and as thou goest
Looke to my flock, and so god speed thee well.

Scæn. 5./ [II. v]

Clarindo . als Siluia sola.

Well, this imployment makes for my avayle,
ffor heereby haue I meanes to see my loue,
who likewise sees me, though hee sees me not,
Nor doo I see him as I would I did.
But I must by some meanes or other make
Him know I live, and yet not so as hee
May know that I am I, for feare wee might
Miscarrie in our ioyes by ouer hast.
But it

985 *als*] *l* crossed through at top with a long stroke (for *alias*)

But it is more then tyme his suffrings were [Fol. 18a]
Releiu'd in some close sort, and that can I devise
No way to doo, but by relating how
I heard of an escape a Nimph did make
ffrom pyrats lately, and was saufe return'd
And so to tell some storie that conteynes
our fortunes and our loues in other names.
And wish him to expect the like event.
ffor I perceiue him very well content
To heare me speake, and sure he hath some note
Although so darkely drawne, as that his eyes
Cannot expressely reade it, yet it shewes
Him something, wch he rather feeles then knowes./

Actus. 3. Scæn. 1. [III. i]

Charinus, the father of Thirsis, Palæmon. /

Palæmon you mee thinks might something worke
wth *Thirsis* my aggreiued sonne, and sound
His humor, what it is, and whie hee thus
Afflicts himself in solitarynes.
You twoe were wont to be most inward frends
And glad I was to see it, knowing you
To be a man well tempred, fitt to sorte
wth his raw youth. can you doo nothing now?
To wyn him home from this captiuitie
of passion, that wthholdes him from the world?

Pal. In troth *Charinus* I haue often tymes
As one that suffred for his greevances

Ass

Fol. 18a] numbered *6* in top right-hand corner 1006–7] pen flourish between these lines
1007] blot at end of line 1010 *wth*] *t* not crossed 1016 *wth*] *t* not crossed

[FOL. 18b]

Assay'd to finde a way into the cause
of his so strange dismay. and by all meanes
Aduis'd him make redemption of himself,
And come to life againe, and be a man
wth men. but all serues not, I finde him lockt
fast to his will. alleadge I what I can.
Cha. But will he not impart to you the cause?
Pal. The cause is loue, but it is such a loue
As is not to be had. *Cha:* not to be had?
Palæmon, if his loue be regular.
Is there in all *Arcadia* any shee
whome his abillitie, his shape, and worth
May not attayne, he beeing my only sonne?
Pal. Shee is not in *Arcadia* whome he loues
Nor in the world, and yett he deerely loues.
Cha. How may that bee *Palæmon*, tell me playne?
Pal. Thus playnely. h'is in loue wth a dead woman.
And that so farr, as wth the thought of her
wch hath shutt out all other. hee alone
Lyues. and abhorres to be, or seene, or knowne.
Cha. What was that creature could possesse him so?
Pal. ffaire *Siluia*, old *Medorus* daughter, who
was twoe yeres past reported to be slayne
By Sauage beasts vpon our Countrey shore
Cha. Is that his greife? alas I rather thought
It appertayn'd vnto anothers part
To wayle her death. *Alexis* should doo that
To whome her father had disposed her
And shee esteemed only to be his.
Whie should my sonne afflict him more for her
Then doth *Alexis*, who this day doth wedd
ffayre *Galatea*, and forgetts the dead.
And heere the shepherds come to celebrate
His

1036 *me*] *e* blotted 1037 *wth*] *t* not crossed 1048 ^{2}*her*] *e* blotted

His ioyfull nuptialls, wth all meryment. [FOL. 19a]
wch doth increase my cares, considering
The comforts other parents doo receiue
And therefore good *Palæmon* worke all meanes
You can to wyn him from his peevish will,
And draw him to theis shewes, to companies
That others pleasures may enkindle his.
And tell him what a syn hee doth com̃ytt
To wast his youth in sollytarynes
And take a course to end vs all in him.

Pal. Assure your self, *Charinus*, as I haue
So will I still imploy my vtmost powre
To saue him. for me thinks it pittie were
So rare a peece of worth should be so lost
That ought to be preseru'd at any cost.

Actus. 3. Scæn. 2. [III. ii]

Charinus. Medorus. |

Medorus come, wee twoe must sitt and mourne,
whilst others revell. wee are not for sports
or nuptiall shewes. wch will but shew vs more
our miseries, in being both depryu'd
The comforts of our issue. wch might haue
(And was as likely to haue made our harts)
As ioyfull now, as others are in theirs.

Med. Indeed *Charinus*, I for my part haue
Iust cause to greiue, amidst theis festiualls
for they should haue bene myne. this day I should
Haue.

1054 *ioyfull*] dot of *i* unusually large 1055 *increase*] ^{1}*e* blotted 1064 *Pal.*] *al* heavily inked
1065 *imploy*] *o* blotted 1068–9] pen flourish between these lines 1080 *for*] *o* has unusual tail

Haue seene my daughter *Siluia* how she would [Fol. 19b]
Haue womand it. theis rytes had bene her grace,
And shee had sate in *Galateas* place.
And now had warm'd my hart to see my bloud
Preseru'd in her. had she not bene so rapt
And rent from of the living as shee was.
But your case is not paralel wth myne
You haue a sonne *Charinus* that doth live
And may one day, to you like comforts giue.
Cha. Indeed I haue a sonne, but yet to say hee lives
I cannot. for who lyves not to the world
nor to himself, cannot be said to liue.
ffor euer since that you your daughter lost
I lost my sonne. for from that day hee hath
Imbrak'd in shades and solytarynes.
Shutt himself vp from sight or companie
of any living. and as now I heard
By good *Palæmon*, vowes still so to doo.
Med. And did your sonne, my daughter loue so deere?
Now good *Charinus* I must greiue the more
Yf more my hart could suffer then it doth.
ffor now I feale the horrour of my deed
In having cross'd the worthiest match on earth.
Now I perceiue whie *Siluia* did refuse
To marry wth *Alexis*, having made
A worthier choice, wch ô had I had grace
To haue foreseene, perhaps this dismall chance
Had never beene. and now they both had had
Ioy of their loues, and wee the like of them.
But ah my gredie eye, viewing the large
And spacious sheepwalks ioyning vnto myne
Wh

1087 *wth*] *t* not crossed 1105 *wth*] *t* not crossed 1108 *both*] *o* blotted

wherof *Alexis* was possest, made mee [Fol. 20a]
As worldlings doo. desire to marry grounds
And not affections, wch haue other bounds.
  How oft haue I wth threats, wth promises,
wth all perswations, wrought to wyn her mynde
To fancye him. yet all would not prevaile.
How oft hath shee againe vpon her knees
wth teares besought mee. ô deere father myne
doo not inforce me to accept a man
I cannott loue. ah rather take from mee
The life you gaue me, then afflict it so.
  Yett all this would not alter myne entent
This was the man shee must affect, or none,
But ah what syn was this to torture so
A hart forevow'd vnto a better choice
where goodnes mett in one the self same point,
And virtues answer'd in an equall ioynt.
  Sure, sure *Charinus* for this syn of myne
The gods bereaft me of my child, and would
not haue her bee, to be wthout her hart,
Nor mee take ioy, where I did none impart.

Cha. *Medorus* thus wee see mans wretchednes
That learnes his errours but by their successe
And when there is no remedie. and now
wee can but wishe it had beene otherwise.

Med. And in that wish *Charinus* wee are rackt
But I remember now I often haue
Had shadowes in my sleepe, that figures bare
of some such liking twixt yor childe and myne.
And this last night a pleasing dreame I had
(Though dreames of ioy, make wakers myndes more sad)

Me.

1115 ^{1}*wth* and ^{2}*wth*] *t* not crossed   1119 *wth*] *t* not crossed   1131 *wthout*] ^{1}*t* not crossed
1134 *their*] *r* altered

Me thought my daughter *Siluia* was return'd [Fol. 20b]
In most strange fashion. and vpon her knees
Craues my goodwill for *Thirsis*, otherwise
Shee would be gone againe, and seene no more.
I at the sight of my dere childe, was rapt
wth that excesse of ioy, as gaue no tyme
Eyther for me to answere her request
or leave for sleepe to figure out the rest.
Cha. Alas *Medorus*, dreames as vapoures, w^{ch}
Ingendred wth day thoughts, fall in the night
And vanishe wth the morning. are but made
Afflictions vnto men, to th'end they might
Not rest in rest, but toyle both day and night.
But see here comes my solitarie sonne
Lett vs stand close *Medorus* out of sight
And note how hee behaues himself in this
Affliction, and distressed case of his. /

Scæn. 3. [III. iii]

Thirsis solus.

This is the day, the lamentable day
of my distruction, wch the Sun hath twice
Return'd vnto my greifes, wch kepe one course
Contynually wth it in motion like,
But that they neuer sett. this day doth clayme
Th'especiall tribuite of my sighes and teares
Though euery day I duely pay my teares
vnto that soule that this day left the world.
And yett I know not whie, me thought the sun
Arose this day wth farr more cherefull rayes
wth

1159–60] pen flourish between these lines

wth brighter beames then vsually it did. [Fol. 21a]
As if it would bring something of release
vnto my cares. or ells my spirit hath had
Some manner of intelligence wth hope
Wherewth my hart is vnacquainted yet.
And that might cause myne eye wth quicker sence
To note thappeering of the eye of heaven.
But something sure I feale wch doth beare vp
The waight of sorrow easier then before /.

Scæn. *4.* [III. iv]

Palæmon. *Thirsis.*/

What *Thirsis*, still in passion? still one man?
ffor shame shew not yor self so weakely sett
So feably ioynted that you cannot beare
The fortunes of the world like other men.
Beleiue me *Thirsis* you much wrong yor worth
This is to be no man, to haue no powres
Passions are womens parts, actions ours.
I was in hope t'haue found you otherwise.
Thi. How? otherwise *Palæmon*? doo not you
Hold it to be a most heroicq*ue* thing
To act one man, and doo that part exact.
Can there be in the worlde more worthines
Then to be constant? Is there any thing
Shewes more a man? what would you haue me change?
That were to haue me base, that were indeed
To

1180–1] pen flourish between these lines neatly scratched out 1195 *any*] *an* blotted 1194 *worlde*] *ld* written over two indecipherable letters, 1197 *indeed*] short horizontal stroke follows

To shew a feeble hart; and weakely sett. [FOL. 21b]
No no *Palæmon*, I should hold my self
The most vnworthie man of men, should I
But lett a thought in to this brest of myne
That might disturbe or shake my constancie.
And thinke *Palæmon*, I haue combats too
To be the man I am, being built of flesh
And having round about me traytors too
That seeke to vndermyne my powres, and steale
Into my weaknesses. but that I kepe
Contynuall watch and ward vpon my self
Least I should be surpriz'd at vnawares
And taken from my vowes. wth other snares.
And even now at this instant I confesse
Palæmon I doo feale. a certeine touch
of comfort, wch I feare to intertayne
Least it should be some spie, sent as a trayne
To make discouerie of what strength I am.

Pal. Ah worthie *Thirsis*, intertayne that spirit
what euer els thou doo. sett all the dores
of thine affections open thervnto.

Thi. *Palæmon* no; Comfort and I haue beene
So long tyme strangers, as that now I feare
To lett him in. I know not how t'acquaint
myself therewth, being vsed to convers
wth other humors, that affect me best.
Nor doo I loue to haue mixt companie
whereto I must of force my self applie.

Pal. But *Thirsis* thinke that this must haue an end
And more it would approue yor worth to make
The same your worke; then tyme should make it his.

Thi. End sure it must *Palæmon*, but with mee:

1228 *worke*] stain above *wo* from ink blot on Fol. 21a (1195 *any*)

ffor so I by the Oracle was told [Fol. 22a]
That verie day wherein I lost the day
And light of comfort that Can never rest
againe to mee, when the saddest [the] man
that ever breath'd, before those Altars fell
And there besought to know what was becom
of my deare *Siluia*, whether dead, or how
Reaft from the world, but that I could not learn
Yet thus much did that voice divine return:
Go youth, reserue thy self the day will come
thou shalt be happie & reioyce againe
But when shall be that day demaunded I
The day thou dyest, replide the *Oracle*
  So that yo^{w} see it will not be in theis
But in the Elizian ffeiles where I shall ioye
The day of death must bring o^{r} happines
Pal. Yo^{w} may mistake the meañing of those words
wch is not known before it be fullfilld
Yeald yo^{w} to what the Gods comãuñd, if not
vnto yor frends desires, reserue yor self
for better dayes, & thinke the *Oracle*
Is not vntrue, although not vnderstood
  But how soever let it not be said
That *Thyrsis* being a man of so rare partes
So vnderstanding & discret should pine in loue
and languish for a silly woman thus
To be the fable of the vulgar, made
a skorn and laught at, by inferior witts
Th. In loue *Palemon*? Know yo^{w} what yo^{w} say?
Can yo^{w} name loue, & not shrinke at y^{t} name?
doe y⟨o⟩^{w} esteeme it light to be in loue?

Fol. 22a] numbered 7 (head cropped) in right-hand corner 1230–1338] transcribed by Hand A 1233 *when*] for *when I* 1239 *will*] loop of ¹*l* blotted 1241 *shall*] loop of ¹*l* blotted 1244 *ffeiles*] for *ffeilds* 1251 *vntrue*] *t* written over *d* 1260 *y⟨o⟩w*] *o* and ascender of *y* blotted and barely legible

[Fol. 22b]

how haue I ben mistaken in the choice
of such a frend as I held yow to be
That seemes not or els doth not vnderstand
the noblest porc̃on of humanity
The worthiest peece of Nature set in man
Ah know that when yo^{w} mention loue, yo^{w} name
A sacred misterie, a dietie
Not vnderstand of creatures buylt of Mud
but of the purest & refyned Clay
where to th'eternall fires them spirits convey
   And for a Woman wch yo^{w} prize so low,
like men that doo forget whence they were men
Know her to be th'especiall Creature, made
by the Creto^{r} as the complement
of this great Architect the world, to hould
The same together wch would other-wise
fall all asunder and is Natures cheif
Vicegerent vpon Earth supplyes her State
   And doo yo^{w} hold it weaknes then to loue?
And loue so excellent a Miracle
as is a worthie woman? ah then let me
still be so weake, Still let me loue & pine
In contemplac̃on of the cleene cleere Soule
That made mine see, that nothing in the world
is so supremely bewtifull as it
   Thinke not it was those Coullo^{rs} *white* & read
layd but on flesh, that could affect me so
But somthing els wch thought holds vnder locke
and hath no key of words to open it
They are the smallest peeces of the mynde
that passe this narrow organ of the voice
The great remain behinde in that vast Orb

1267 *dietie*] ^{1}*i* not dotted; for *deitie* 1268 *vnderstand*] for *vnderstood* 1277 *asunder*] written as *a sunder* 1291 *voice*] *o* touched up or blotted 1292 *behinde*] written as *be hinde* *that*] stain below ^{1}*t* from ink blot on Fol. 22a (1260 *y*⟨*o*⟩*w*)

of th'apprehension & are never borne [FOL. 23a]
And therefore if yor Iudgement cannot reach
vnto the vnderstanding of my case
Yo^{w} doo not well to put yor self into
my Iurie to condemne ⌜me⌝ as yo^{w} doo
let th'ignorant out of their dulnes laugh
At thee my suffrings, I will pittye them
To haue ben so ill borne, so miscompos'd
as not to know what thing it is to loue
And I to great *Apollo* here appeale
The Sou'raign of the Muses, & of all
well tun'd affections, & to *Cynthia* bright
& glorious Lady of cleere faithfullnes
whoe from aboue looke down wth blissfull beames
vpon o^{r} hum'ble Groves, & ioy the harts
of all the world to see their naturall loues
They can best iudge what worthines there is
in worthy loue, Therefore *Palemon* peace
vnlesse yo^{w} did know better what it were.
And this be sure, when that fire goes out
in Man, hee is the miserablest thing
on Earth, his daylight sets, and is all darke
and dull wthin, no motions of delight
But all opprest lyes struggling w^{t} the weight
of worldly cares, and this old *Damon* sayes
who well had felt what loue was in [t]his dayes
Pal. Well *Thyrsis* well how ever yo^{w} doe guild
Yo^{wr} passions to indeere them to yor selfe
Yo^{w} never shall induce me to beleeue
That sicknesses can be of such effect
And so farwell, vntill yo^{w} shall be well.

1294 *yor*] raised *r* written over raised *w* *reach*] *r* resembles *E* 1297 *me*] interlined above a caret 1299 *thee*] for *these* 1304 *tun'd*] *n* heavily inked 1305 *faithfullnes*] written as *faith fullnes* 1316 *struggling*] *u* altered from *o* 1319 *Thyrsis*] *r* added above *ys* 1320 *to indeere*] ink smudges around these words

Scen. 5. [III. v] [Fol. 23b]

Medorus. Charimus.

O Gods *Charimus* what a man is this
whoe ever heard of such a constancie
had I but known him in inioying him
as now I doo, to liue, in loosing him
how that had bene mine age, but ah I was
vnworthie of so great a blessedness
Cha. yo^{w} see *Medorus* how no Councell can
prevaile to turne the Current of his will
to make it run in anie other course
then what it doth so that I see I must
Esteeme him irrecoverably lost
But hearke the Shepheards festivalls begin
let vs from hence where sadnes were a syn.

1326 *Charimus*] *i* touched up 1334 *run*] *u* altered from *a* 1338 *syn.*] flourish above full stop

[Fol. 24a]

The third Song.

from the temple to the borde
from the bord vnto the bed
we conduct yor Maydenhead
wishing Hymen to afford
All the pleasures y^{t} he can
Twixt a woman and a man.

So merely we pass along
w^{t} o^{r} ioyfull bridall Song

1339–47] transcribed by Daniel

Actus 4. Scen. 1. [IV. i] [Fol. 24b]
Thyrsis. Solus.

I thought these simple woods, these gentle Trees
would in regard, I ame their dayly guest
& harbo^{r} vnderneath their shadie roofes
not haue consented to delude my griefes
& mocke my miseries wth false reports
But now I see they will afflict me too
    for as I cam by yonder spreading Beach
wch often hath the Secretary bene
to my sad thoughts, while I haue rested me
if loue had ever rest) vnder his gentle shade
I found incarv'd & faire incarv'd theas words
Thy Syluia, Thyrsis, liues, and is returnd
Ah me that any hand would thus ad skorn
vnto affliction, & a hand so faire
as this may seeme to be, wch were more fit
m[y]e thinks for good, then to doo iniuery
for sure no virtue should be ill imployd
    And wch is more, the name of Siluia was
Carv'd in the selfe same kinde of Character
wch she aliue did vse, and where wth all
subscribd her [woyes] ⌜vowes⌝ to me, who knowes it best
wch shewes the frende the more, & more the wrong
Therefore yo^{w} Starres of that hight Court of Heven

1348–1910] transcribed by Hand A   1349 *Thyrsis*] to the left, a headstroke of *I*, suggesting false start for 1350   1355 *will*] loop of ¹*l* blotted   1359 *if*] for *(if*   1365 *m[y]e*] *e* interlined above deletion   1368 *same*] *m* dotted   *Character*] *cte* touched up   1370 *vowes*] interlined above deletion   1371 *shewes*] ²*e* blotted or altered   *frende*] ¹*e* altered from *a*   *wrong*] *r* altered, *o* touched up   1372 *hight*] *t* may be crossed through for deletion

wch doo reveale deceipts, & punish them, [Fol. 25a]
let not this crime to counterfet a hand
to cozen my desires escape yor doome
nor let these Ryotts of intrusion, made
vpon my lonenes by strange company
afflict me thus, but let me haue some rest
  Come thou refressher of all living things
Soft sleepe, come gently, & take truce wth these
Oppresso^{rs} but com simplie & alone
w^{t}out those Images of fantasie
wch hurt me more then thou canst doo me good
let me not sleepe, vnlesse I could sleepe all

Scen^{a}. 2. [IV. ii]
Palæmon. Thyrsis.

Alas he heere hath lay'd him down to rest
it weere now Sin his quiet to molest
And God forbed I should, I will retire
& leaue him, for I know his greifes require
This poore relieum^{t}. of a little sleepe
Th. what Spirit here haunts me now? what no time free?
Ah is it yo^{w} *Palæmon*? would to god
yo^{w} would forbeare me but a little while
Yo^{w} shew yor care of me too much in this
vnseasonable loue ⌜scarce⌝ kindenes is
Pal. Good *Thyrsis* I ame sorrie I should giue
the least occasion of diseas to yo^{w}
I will be gon, & leaue yo^{w} to yor rest

1374 *crime*] *i* altered 1375 *escape*] *c* altered from *t* 1380 *truce*] *c* interlined above *ue*
1396 *scarce*] interlined above a caret, between *loue* and *kindenes*

Th. doo good *Palemon* go yor way, fare well [Fol. 25b]
And yet *Palemon* stay, perhaps yo^{w} may
by charmes yo^{w} haue cause sleepe to close mine eyes
for yo^{w} were wont, I doo remember well
To sing me Sonnets wch in passion I
Compos'd in my happier dayes when as
her beames inflam'd my Spirits, wch now ar set
And if yo^{w} can remember it, I pray
Sing me the Song, wch thus begins: *Eyes hide my loue,*
wch I did write vppon the earnest Charge
she gaue vnto me to conceale o^{r} loue

The Song. *Eyes hide my loue, and doo not shew*
to anie but to her my notes
who onely doth that Cypher know
wherewth wee pass our secret thoughts
bely your lookes in others sight
and wrong yor.selues to doo her right

Pal. So now hee sleepes, or els doth seeme to sleepe
But how soe're I will not troble him

Scen. 3. [IV. iii]
Clarindo. Thyrsis.

See where hee lyes whome I so long to see
Ah my deare *Thyrsis* take thie quiet rest
I know thou needst it, sleepe thy fill, sweet loue
let. nothing trouble thee: be c[l]alme ô windes
Bee[⟨.⟩] still yo^{w} Heards, chirp not to lowd sweet Birds
least yo^{w} should wake my loue, thou gentle Bancke

1401 *Palemon*] *e* oddly formed 1404 *Sonnets*] *e* added above *nt* 1425 *sweet*] *s* written over *f*

that thus art blest to beare so deare a waight [Fol. 26a]
Be soft vnto those daintie limmes of his
ply tender grass, and render sweete refresh
vnto his weary sences whilest hee rests.
  O could I now but put of this disguise
wth those respects that fetter my desire
how closelie could I neighbo^{r} that sweete side
But stay. hee stirrs, I fear my hart hath brought
my feet to neere, & I haue wakened him
Th. It will not be, sleep is no frend of mine
Or such a frend as leaues a man, when most
hee needes him, See a new assault. who now
Ah tis the Boy that was w^{t} me erwhiles
That gentle Boy, I ame content to speake
wth him, hee speakes so pretely, so sweete
And wth so good respectiue modesty
and well resembles one I know over well
Come hether gentle Boy w^{hat} hast thou there?
Cla. A token sent yo^{w} from the nimphe I serue,
Th. Keepe it my Boy, & weare it on thy head
Cla. The Gods forbid that I a servant should
wear on my head, that wch my mistress hath
prepar'd for yo^{rs}. S^{r}. I beseche yo^{w} vrge
no more a thing so ill becoming me
Th. Nay sure I thinke it better will becom
thy head then mine & therefore Boy thou must
needes put it on *Cla.* I trust yor lonenes hath not
vncivilld yo^{w} to force a messinger
to doo against good mañners, & his will
Th. no, good my Boy, but I intreat the now

1429 *and*] mark before *a* is showthrough from Fol. 26b   1444 *w^{hat}*] *hat* touched up
1453 *not*] followed by vertical stroke at edge of page

[FOL. 26b]

let me but put it on, hold still thy head
It shall not be thie Art, but onely mine
let it alone good Boy, for if thou sa'wist
how well it did become thee sure thou wouldst
Now, canst thou sing my Boy, some gentle Song?
Cla. I cannot sing, but I could weepe. *Thyr.* wep, whie?
Cla. Because I ame not as I wishe to bee
Th. why so are none, be not displeas'd for that
And if yo^{w} cannot sing, tell me some Tale
to passe the time. *Cla.* that can I doo.
did I but know what kinde of Tale yo^{w} like
Th. No merry tale my Boy, nor yet to sad;
But mixed like the Tragicq*ue* Com̃edie
Cla. Then such a tale I haue, and a true tale.
Beliue me S^{r} although not written yet
In any booke, but sure it will I know
some gentle shepherd mov'd w^{t} passion must
Record it to the world, and well it will
Become the world to vnderstand the same.
And this it is. There was somtymes a nimph
[I]Sulia name'd, and an *Arcadian* born:
ffayre can I not avouch she was, but chaste
And honest sure, as the event will prove.
whose mother dying leaft her very young
vnto her fathers chardg, who carefully
did breed her vp, vntill she came to yeares
of womanhood, and then provides a match
Both rich, and yong and fit ynough for her

1457 *head*] *e* added above *ha*, *d* written over *r* 1458 *onely*] *n* has three minims, the last blotted 1473 *shepherd*] [1]*e* altered from *a* 1477 *[I]Sulia*] deletion preceded by another letter, perhaps *I*, scratched out; for *Isulia* 1478 *ffayre*] *ff* written over indecipherable deletion 1483 *womanhood*] written as *woman hood* *provides*] *s* written over *d*

[Fol. 27a]

But she who to another shepheard had,
Calld Syrthis, vow'd her loue, as vnto one
Her hart esteem'd more worthy of her love
Could not by all her ffathers meenes be wrought
To leave her choyce, and to forgo her vow
Th. no more could my deare Siluia be from me
Cla. wc caused much affliction to them both.
Th. And So the self same cause did vnto vs
Cla. This nimph one day, surchardg'd wt love and grief
wc comonly (the more the pitty) dwell
As Inmat's both together, walking forth
wt other maydes to fish vppon the shore
Estrayes a part and leaves her company
To intertayn her self wt her own thoughts.
And wanders on so far, and out of sight
As she at length was sodaynly Surpris'd
By Pyrats who lay lucking vnderneath
Those hollow rocks, expecting there some prive
And not wt standing all her pittious cryes
Intreaty teares, and prayers. those fierce men
Rent hayre, and vayle, and carryed her by force
Into their ship wc in a little Creeke
Hard by, at Anker lay. and prsently hoysd sayle
And so away. *Th*: Rent hayre and vayle? and so,
Both hayre and vayle of Siluia I found rent
wc here I keepe wt me. but now alas
what did shee? what became of her my boy
Cla. when she was thus inship'd and wofully
Had cast her eyes about to view that Hell

1495 *Inmat's*] *s* written over ?*d* *together*] written as *to gether* 1497 *Estrayes*] 2*s* written over *d*
1501 *lucking*] for *lurking* 1502 *prive*] for *prize*

[FOL. 27b]

of horror, where in to she was so sodaynly
Implung'd: she spyes a woman sitting w^{t} a child
⌜sucking her brest. w^{c} was the captaynes wife⌝
To her she creepes, down at her fet she ly'd:
O woman if y^{t} name of woman, may
move yo^{w} to pitty, pitty a pore mayd.
The most distressed soule that ever breathd
And save mee from the hands of these fierce men.
let mee not be defilde and [I] made vncleene
deare woman now and I wilbee to yo^{w}
The faithfullst slave that ever mistrisse serv'd
never pore soule shalbe more duty-full
To doo what ever yo^{w} com̃and then I.
no toyle will I refuse so y^{t} I may
keepe this poore bodie cleene and vndeflowr'd,
w^{c} is all I will ever seeke. for know
It is not feare of death layed mee thus low
But of that stayne will make my death to blush
Th. what would not all this move the womans hart
Cla. All this could nothinge move the womans hart
whom yet. she would not leave but still besought
O woman by that infant at yo^{w} brest
And by the paynes it cost yo^{w} in the birth
Saue mee, as ever yo^{w} desyre to have
yo^{w} babe to ioy and prosper in the world
w^{c} will the better prosper [m] Sure, if yo^{w}
shall mercy shew w^{c} is w^{t} mercy pay'd.
Then kisses she her feet. then kisses too
the infants feet, and O sweet babe sayd she

1516] interlined after transcription of 1515 and 1517   1516 *w^{c}*] raised *c* above indecipherable letter   1522 *[I]*] neatly scratched out (eyeslip for 1523 *I*)   *1524 *serv'd*] added later   1527 *toyle*] *o* touched up   1532 *all*] *a* altered   1535 *yo^{w}*] for *yor*   1538 *yo^{w}*] for *yor*   1539 *[m]*] neatly scratched out (?eyeslip for 1540 ²*mercy*)

[Fol. 28a]

couldst thou but to thy mother speake for mee
And crave her to have pittie on my cast.
Thou might'est p*er*haps p^{r}vayle w^{t} her so much
Although I cannot, chide. ah couldst thou speake
The Infant whether by her touching it
Or by imstinct of nature, seeing her weep
lookes earnestly vppon her, and then lookes
vppon the mother: then on her againe,
And then it cryes, and then on either lookes
w^{c} she p*er*ceuing. blessed childe sayd shee
Although thou canst not speak, yet dost thou cry
vnto thy mother for mee. heare thy childe
Deare mother, it's for mee it Cryes.
It's all the speach it hath. accept those cryes
Saue mee at his request from beeing defylde.
let pitty move thee y^{t} thus moves thy childe.
The woman, though by birth and Custome rude
yet having vaynes of nature, could not bee
But pierceble, did fele at length the poynt
of pittie enter so, as out gusht teares,
(not vsuall to stirn eyes) and she besought
Her husband to bestow on her that prive
w^{t} safegard of her bodie; at her will.
The captayn seeing his wife, his child, the nimph
All crying to him in this pittious sort
felt his rough nature shaken too. and grants
His wifes request and Seales his grant w^{t} teares.
And so they wept all foure for company

Fol. 28a] numbered *8* in top right-hand corner 1544 *cast*] for *case* 1548 *imstinct*] for *instinct*
1555 *Deare*] *D* altered 1563 *stirn*] *i* made out of *?e* *besought*] written as *be sought*
1564 *prive*] for *prize* 1566 *captayn*] *p* written over *t*

[Fol. 28b]

And some beholders stood not wt dry eyes
such passion wrought, the passion of their prive.

Th. In troth my boy, and even thy telling it
moues mee like wise, thou dost so feallingly,
Report the same as yf thou hadst ben by
But I imagine now how this poore nimph
when she receiued that doome was comforted

Cla. Sr. never was there pardon that did take
condemned from the block, more ioyfull then
This grant to her. for all her misery
seem'd nothing to the comfort she received
By beeing thus saved from impuritie
And from the womans feet she would not part
nor trust her hand to be wtout some hold
of her, or of her child so long as she remayn'd
wt in the ship, wc in few dayes arived
At Alexandria whence these pyrats were.
And there this wofull mayd for two yeares space
did serve and truly serv'd this captaynes wife
who would not lose the benifit of her
Attendance, for her prefit other wise.
But daring not in such a place as that
To trust her self in womans habit, crav'd
That she might be apparell'd, as a boy:
And so she was, and as a boy she serv'd,

Th. And two yeares t[o]'is since I my Siluia lost

Cla. At two yeares end, her mistres sends her forth
vnto the Port for some comodities;
wc whilst she Sought for, going vp and downe

1572 *prive*] for *prize* 1577 *receiued*] 2*e* dotted 1591 *prefit*] for *profit* 1596 *And*] written over ink smudge 1599 *going*] ink smudge through *n*

she heard some merchants men of Corinth talke, [FOL. 29a]
who speake that language the Arcadians did,
And were next neigbors of one continent.
To them all rapt w^c passion downe she kneeles
Tells them she was a pore distressed boy
Borne in Arcadia, and by pyrats tooke
And made a slave in Egipt: and besought
Them, as they fathers were of children, or
did hold their natiue country deare they would
Take pitty on her, and release her youth
from y^t sad servitude wherein she liud;
for w^c she hop'd that she had freinds aliue
would thanke them, one day, and reward them too
if not, yet that, she knew, the heavens would doo
   The Marchants mov'd w^t pittie of her case
Beeing ready to depart tooke her w^t them,
And landed her vppon her country Cost.
where when she found her self, she prostrate falles
Kisses the ground, thankes giues vnto the godds,
Thankes them who had bene her deliverars.
   And on she trudges thorow deseart woods
Clymes over craggy rocks, and mountayns as steep.
wades thorow ryvers r struggles thorow bogges
sustayned onely by the force of love
vntill she came vnto the native Playnes
vnto the feilds, where first she drew her breath
   There lifts she vp her eyes salutes the ayre
Salutes the trees, the bushes, flowres and all.

1600 *merchants*] *r* added above *ec*; for *merchante*   **talke,*] comma added in lighter brown ink
1603 *w^c*] for *w^t*   1616 *Cost*] *Co* blotted and touched up   1622 *r*] for *&*

And o deare Syrthis, here I ame, Saide shee [FOL. 29b]
Here, not w^{t} standing all my miseries
I ame the same I was to thee. a pure
A chast a spotles mayde. o that I may
finde thee the man, thou didst profess to bee,
Th. Or els no man, for, boy, who truly loves
must ever so. that dye will never out
And who but would love truly such a Soule?
Cla. But now the better to have notice how
The state of thinges then stood; and not in haste
To cast her self on new incombrances
The kept her habit still, and put her selfe
To serve a nimph of whom she had made choyce
Till tyme were fitting to reveale her self
Th. This may be Siluias case. this may be she
But is it not? let me consider well.
The tellar, and the circumstance agree,

Scen. 3. [IV. iv]
Montanus. Thyrsis. Chorus.

Ah Sirrha. have I found yo^{w}? are yo^{w} heare
yo^{w} princock boy? and w^{t} yo^{w} garland on.
do this attyre become yo^{w} peevish head?
Com I must teach yo^{w} better manners, boy.
He stabbs Clarindo and russhes of his Garland.
So, Phillis I haue donne my task, and here
I bring the Trophey to confirm the same

1632 *didst*] ^{2}*d* added above *s* 1636 *notice*] *n* altered from *m* 1638 *incombrances*] written as *incombrances* 1639 *The*] for *She* 1644 *the*] smudged 1645 *3*] for *4* 1648 ^{2}*yo^{w}*] for *yor* 1649 *yo^{w}*] for *yor* 1650 *must*] *t* smudged

Thou shalt not now, need feere, nor bragges, nor tale [FOL. 30a]
Th. Ah monster man, vile wretch, what hast thou don.
Alas, in what a straight am I ingaged heare?
yf I parsue revenge I leave to save.
Help, healp. you gentle Swaynes, if any now be ⌜nea⟨r⟩⌝
Help, healp. ah hearke. even eccho helps me to cry help
Cho. what meanes this outcry. Sure some savage beast
disturbs o^{r} heards. or els some wolf hath seez'd
vppon a lamb. Thyr. A worse thing then a wolfe
more blody then a beast, hath murthred here
A gentle creature then a lambe. therefore
Good Swayne pursue, persue the homicide.
That ougly wretch Montanus, who hath stabbd
This Sealy creture heare, at vnawares.
Montanus? why, we me't him but even now.
Deckt w^{t} a garland, grumbling to him selfe
We will attach that villayn p^{r}sently
Come Sirs make hast. and let vs after him

Sen. 4. [IV. v]
Palemon. Thyrsis.

Alas what accident is here faln out?
my deare freind Thyrsis how comes this to passe
Th. That monster man Montanus, here hath stabbd
A harmles youth in message sent to mee

1655 *monster*] *n* added above *os* space at the edge of the page) 1658 *nea⟨r⟩*] interlined, with a caret, above *be* (because of lack of space at the edge of the page) 1664 *gentle*] for *gentler* 1668] speech-prefix *Cho.* omitted 1672 *Sen.4*] for *Scen.5*

now good Palæmon help me hold him vp. [Fol. 30b]
And see if that we can recover him.
Pal. It may be Thyrsis, more his feare then hart
stay him a while, and I will haste, and seas
for lamia, who w^{t} oyntments, oyls and herbs
if any help remayne will help him sure.
Th. do good Palæmon, make what haste yo^{w} may.
Seeke out for help, and be not long away.
Alas sweete boy that thou shouldst ever have
So hard misfortune com̃ing vnto mee.
And end thy tale w^{t} this sad tragidie,
That tale w^{c} will resembled Siluias case
w^{c} thou resemblest, for Such browes had shee.
such a proportion'd face, and such a necke.
What have we here, the mole of Siluia too?
What? and her brests? what? and her hayre, what? all
All Siluia? yes, all Siluia, and all dead
And art thou thus returnd agayne to mee?
Art thou thy self that strange deliucred nimph?
And didst thou come to tell me thy escape
from death to dy before mee? had I not
ynough to doo, to wa'yle reported harmes,
But thou must come to bleed w^{t} in myne armes?
was not one death sufficient for my griefes
But that thou must dy twice? why thou wert dead

1681 *seas*] *s* perhaps *d*; for *send* *1688 *tragidie,*] comma added in lighter brown ink 1689 *will*] for *well* 1690 *w*^{c}] raised *c* written over *e*, scratched out *1691 *proportion'd*] apostrophe perhaps added in lighter brown ink *1693 *What?*] *?* written over stop in lighter brown ink 1694 ^{1}*Siliua*] *l* heavily inked *1695 *mee?* *1696 *nimph?*] *?* written over stop in lighter brown ink 1696 *deliucred*] for *deliuered* *1699 *harmes,*] comma added in lighter brown ink 1700 *myne armes*] smudged in places

To me before? why? must thou dy agayne? [FOL. 31a]
Ah better had it bene still to be lost
Then thus to haue ben found. yet better found
Though thus. then so lost as was thought before,
for how soever now I have thee yet
thogh in the saddest fashion that may bee:
yet Siluia now I haue thee, and will I
no more for ever part w^{t} thee agayne.
And we this benefit shall have thereby,
Though fate would not p*er*mit vs both to have
One bed, yet, Siluia, we shall have one grave:
And that is somthing, and much more then I
Expected ever could haue come to pass.
And sure the godds but onely sent thee thus
To fetch mee, and to take me hence w^{t} thee
And Siluia so thou shalt. I ready ame
T'accompany thy soule, and that w^{t} speed.
The strings, I feele. are all dissolu'd, that held
This wofull hart; reserv'd it seemes for this
And well reservd for this so dere an end

Scen.5. [IV. vi]
Chorus. Palæmon.

So we have tooke the villayn, and him bound
fast to an Oake as rugged as him selfe.
And there he stares, and gapes, in th' ayre, and rave⟨s⟩

1704 *better*] loop of *b* blotted 1708 *fashion*] *i* double dottted *1711 *thereby,*] comma added in lighter brown ink 1719 *soule*] *s* written over indecipherable letter 1723 *5*] for *6* *1727 *stares, and*] comma added in lighter brown ink by another hand, which wrote *and* over two indecipherable letters, and which also added a comma in the same ink after *th' ayre* 1727 *rave⟨s⟩*] letter lost at the edge of the page (1615: *raues*)

like a wild beast that's taken in the toyle. [Fol. 31b]
And so he shall remayne, till tyme we see
what will become of this his savage act.

Pal. Cheere Thyrsis, lamia will come presently
And bring the best p^{r}servatiues she hath
what now? who lyes discovred here? aye mee,
A woman dead? Is this that boy transformd?
why this is Siluia? o good Thyrsis how
comes this to pass? freind Thyrsis [s] *Thyrsis* speeke.
Good *Thyrsis* tell mee. out alas he sownes,
As well as she, and both seeme gone alike.
Come gentle herdsmen, come and carry them
To yonder shepcot quickly, that we may
(Yf possible) recover them agayne,
if not p*er*forme those rites that appertayne
vnto so rare a couple, come my frinds, o make haste.

*1728 *that's*] italic *s* written over secretary *s* (letter shape '6') by another hand, which added the apostrophe
*1734 *transformd?*] *?* added over stop in lighter brown ink
*1736 *speeke.*] stop added in lighter brown ink
*1737 *sownes,*] comma added in lighter brown ink
*1740 *shepcot*] *e* altered from *i* by another hand
*1741 *agayne,*] comma added in lighter brown ink
1743 *frinds*] *s* written later, merged with *d*

[Blank] [Fol. 32a]

Fol. 32a] numbered *9* in top right-hand corner

Act. 5. Scen.1. [V. i] [FOL. 32b]

Chorus. Palæmon.

Did ever yet *Arcadia* here before
of two so worthie *Louers* as we finde
Thyrsis & Siluia were ? or ever heard
cleere truth. & simple constant honesty
so lamentable an event as this ?
But here comes forth Palemon we shall now
learn all of him what hath bene doñe wthin
Pal. Go Pollio sommon all th'Arcadian youth
here round about, & will them to p^{r}pare
To celebrate w^{t} all delights they can
this ioyfull howre that hath restor'd to vs
the worthiest paire of harts that ever were
will them to shew the higth of musiq*ue* art
And all the straynes of cuñing they can shew
that we may make theies Rocks & Hills about
Ring w^{t} the Eccho of redoubled notes
And will Charimes & medorus to
the aged Parents of theis worthy paire
To come w^{t} speed, whose ioy, good Soules wilbe
more then their speed & yet their speed I know
wilbe beyond th'allowance of their years
when they shall vnderstand this happie newes
And sommon likewise all the trayne of Nimph
that glorify o^{r} playnes, & all that can
geue hono^{r} to this day
Go Pollio hast a way & as yo^{w} goe
vnbinde Montanus that rude savage Swayne
[⟨And though he be vnwarthie to be heare⟩]

1754 *about*] written as *a bout* 1764 *come*] *om* touched up; signs of scratching out (also around 1765 *then*), but no deletions visible 1766 *th'allowance*] ink mark above *a* *1773] line crossed through with two or three horizontal strokes in the brown ink used by the italic hand which altered 1774; lower half or more of the words was lost when the page was cropped

[Yet] ⌜*And*⌝ let him come, hee hath bene in his dayes [Fol. 33a]
held a good fellow, how soever now
his rage and loue transported him in this
Clo. Palæmon we are glad to see yo^{w} thus
delightfull, now we hope there is good newes,
Pal. Good newes my frends, & I will tell it you
Siluia & Thyrsis being to my Cottage brought
the skillfull Lamia comes & searcht the wound
wch Siluia had receu'd of this rude Swayne
And finding it not deadly she applyde
those remedies she knew of best effect
And bindes it vp, & powres into her mouth
such cordiall waters as reviue the Spirits
And s⟨o⟩ much wrought as she at length p*er*ceiu'd
life was not quite gone out, but lay opprest
wth like indeavo^{rs} wee on *Thyrsis* worke
And mynistred like Cordialls vnto him
At lengh wee might heere Siluia fetch a grone
and therewthall Siluia p*er*ceiu'de to mooue
Then Thyrsis fet a groone, & Siluia mou'd
As if their lives were made both of one peece
whereat wee ioy'd, & then remou'd & sat
each before other & heald vp their heads
And chaff'd their temples, rubb'd, & strok'd their Cheeke⟨s⟩
where wth Siluia first cast vp her dym eyes
And p^{r}sently did Thyrsis lift vp his
and then againe they both together sigh'd
And each on other fixt an vnseeing eye
for yet t'was scarce the twilight of their new
Returning day, out of the night of death
And though [⟨.⟩] they saw, they did not yet p*er*ceaue

Fol. 33a] numbered *10* in top right-hand corner *1774 *And*] interlined above deletion of *Yet* in italic hand, with a caret *1775 *fellow,*] comma added by another hand, in the ink of 1774 *And* 1777 *Clo.*] for *Cho.* 1778 *delightfull*] written as *delight full* **newes,*] comma added by another hand, probably in the ink of 1774 *And* 1787 *s⟨o⟩*] *o* scratched away, perhaps after blotting (a stain remains) 1789 *indeavo^{rs}*] *v* written over *t* 1791 *lengh*] for *length* 1794 *lives*] *v* dotted 1803 *Returning*] *i* altered from *e*

each other, & yet both turnd to one point [FOL. 33b]
As toucht alike, & held their lookes direct
At length we might p*er*ceiue, as life began
T'appeare & make the morning in their eyes
Their beames waxt cleerer. &   looks
did shew as if they tooke some little note
of each the other, yet not so as they
could thorowly discearn who them selues were
  And then wee tooke & ioynd their hands in one
And held eav them so a while, vntill we felt
how eaven each others touch the motion gaue
vnto their feeling, & they trembling wronge
their hands together, & so held them lockt
loo'ke still vppon each other, but no words at all
  Then we coll'd out to Thyrsis looke
It is thy Siluia thou here holdst, she is
Return'd, reviu'd & safe Siluia behold thou hast
Thy Thyrsis, and shalt ever haue him thine
  Then did we set them both vpon their feete
And there they stood in act eaven as before
looking vpon each other hand in hand
At last we saw a blusshing red appeere
in both their Cheeks wch sence sent vs a lampe
To light their vnderstanding. & forth wth
the tears gusht from their eyes, wch hindred them
a while from seeing each other, till they had
Cleer'd them againe, & then as if new wak'd
from out a fearfull dreame they stand & doubt
whether thy were awake in deede, or els
Still in a dreame, distrusting their owne eyes
their long-indur'd miseries would not

1809 *Their*] *r* resembles *n*   *& looks*] space between these for two words (1615: *their opener*)
1814 *eav*] not deleted (eyeslip for 1815 *eaven*)   1827 *vs*] for *as*   1833 *thy*] for *they*; head of *y* touched up

let them beleeue their suddaine happines [FOL. 34a]
Although they saw it, till wth much adoo
they had confirm'd their credit, & had kist
each other, & imbrac'd, & kist againe
And yet still dombe their ioy now seemd to be
to busie wth their thoughts t'allow them words
   And then they walk a little, then stood still
Then walkt againe, & still held either fast
as if they feard, they should be lost againe
And when at last they spake it was but thus,
O Siluia, and O Thyrsis, & there stop.
   We least o^{r} sight & p^{r}sence (being then
So many) hinder might the passage of
their modest, simple, & vnpractizd loue
came all o^{r} way, & onely *Lamia* left
Whose spirit, & that sufficient still she hath
Will serue no doubt to see they shall doo well
Cho. Well may they doo deare cowple who haue thus
grac'd o^{r} *Arcadia* wth their faithfullnes.

Fol. 34a] numbered *11* in top right-hand corner   1842 *walk*] for *walkt*   1848 *might*] *mi* has three minims only   1851 *still*] for *skill*   1853 *cowple*] *w* added above *op*   1854 *Arcadia*] *c* dotted   *faithfullnes.*] written as *faith fullnes.*, followed by horizontal squiggle, resembling *m*

[Blank]

Scen.2. [V. ii] [FOL. 35a]

Phillis. Lidia. Cloris.

What shall ⌜we⌝ now doo *Lidia* ? now am I
vtterly sham'd, this youth turnd yoman is,
Clarindo Siluia is become how now
Can I for ever looke on her againe
or com in any Company for shame ?
now must I needes be made a comon iest
& laughing stocke to every one that shall
but heare how grossly I behaue'd my self
Lid. ffaith Phillis as it is falln out yor case
is very crazie, and to make it whoole
there is no way but even to laugh it out
And set as good a face as yo^{w} may doo
vppon the matter, & say thus, how yo^{w}
knew well enough it was no man whom yo^{w}
affected so, who never could loue man
nor ever would, & that by meere
and sympathie of Sex, yo^{w} fancied him
So put it off, & turn it to a iest.
Ph. That shall I never doo, but ever blush
at her, to thinke what she will thinke of me
who did bewray my selfe so foolishlie
Lid. Are yo^{w} here *Cloris* yo^{w} are blest today
for being mistress vnto such a Boy
yo^{w} may reioice that ever this fell out
Clo. Reioyce ? *ah Lidia* never was there Nimph
had more occasion to be said then I
for I ame quite vndone & sham'd hereby

Fol. 35a] numbered *12* in top right-hand corner 1857 *we*] interlined above a caret, between *shall* and *now* 1858 *yoman*] for *woman*; *a* blotted 1861 *com*] *o* altered from *a* 1870 *whom*] *o* blotted 1872 *meere*] for *meere instinct* 1873 *sympathie*] *a* added above *pt* 1878 *today*] written as *to day* 1882 *occasion*] ^{1}*o* altered from *a* *said*] dot of *i* obscured by ascender of *d*; for *sad* 1883 *sham'd*] *m* dotted

for I imployed this my supposed Boy [Fol. 35b]
In message vnto Thyrsis whome I lov'd
I must confesse, more dearly then my life
And tould him all the secrets of my hart
& therefore wth what face can ever I
looke vppon them that know thus much by mee?
No *Lidia*, I will now take Thyrsis course
hide me for ever in these desert woods
and never come in Company againe
They shall not laught at me in their great ioyes
Lid. But *Cloris* I would laugh at them were I as yo^{w}
& howsoeu*er* felt my self wthin,
Yet would I seeme be otherwise wthout
Cannot yo^{w} say yo^{w} know well enough
how it was Siluia that yo^{w} intertaynd
Although yo^{w} would not seeme to take such note
and therevpon imployd her in that sort
To Thyrsis, knowing who it was would giue
to him the greatest comfort vppon Earth
And thus faire nymphes yo^{w} fitly may excuse
these simple slipps, & know y^{t} they shall still
haue crosses wth their piles who thus do play
there fortunes wth their loues, as yo^{w} two did
But yo^{w} must frame yor countenance thereto
and looke wth other face then their own
As many els doo heere who in their parts
set shyning lookes vpon their cloudy harts. /

1893 *laught*] for *laugh*   1910 *shyning*] *n* added above *yi*

[Blank] [Fol. 36a]

[BLANK] [FOL. 36b]

[BLANK]

[Blank] [Fol. 37b]